Milestones Ⓐ

Workbook
with Test Preparation

HEINLE
CENGAGE Learning™

Australia • Brazil • Japan • Korea • Mexico • Singapore • Spain • United Kingdom • United States

HEINLE
CENGAGE Learning™

Milestones A Workbook with Test Preparation

Editorial Director: Joe Dougherty

Publisher: Sherrise Roehr

Managing Editor: Carmela Fazzino-Farah

Associate Development Editor: Stephen Greenfield

Technology Development Editor: Debie Mirtle

Executive Marketing Manager: Jim McDonough

Director of Product Marketing: Amy T. Mabley

Product Marketing Manager: Katie Kelley

Assistant Marketing Manager: Andrea Bobotas

Director of Content and Media Production: Michael Burggren

Production Assistant: Mark Rzeszutek

Manufacturing Manager: Marcia Locke

Development Editor: Arley Gray

Composition and Project Management: MPS Limited, A Macmillan Company

Interior Design: Rebecca Silber

Cover Design: Page 2, LLC

Cover Image: Darrell Gulin/Corbis

Photo Credits:
p.171, Superstock, Inc./Superstock
p.131, courtesy of Tamim Ansary
p.253 example, Doug Steley / Alamy; item 1, Chris Pancewicz / Alamy; item 2, Lewis Wickes Hine, Bettman / Corbis

ISBN-13: 978-1-4240-2744-6

ISBN-10: 1-4240-2744-6

Heinle
20 Channel Center Street
Boston, MA 02210
USA

Cengage Learning is a leading provider of customized learning solutions with office locations around the globe, including Singapore, the United Kingdom, Australia, Mexico, Brazil, and Japan. Locate your local office at: **international.cengage.com/region**

Cengage Learning products are represented in Canada by Nelson Education, Ltd.

Visit Heinle online at **elt.heinle.com**

Visit our corporate website at **www.cengage.com**

Printed in the United States of America
6 7 8   13 12

Contents

Assessment Practice

Strategies for Testing Success

Good readers will develop many different reading skills. To become a good reader, you will need to learn to read different kinds of texts. Many tests measure your reading skills. You will soon take one of these tests. The test will ask many questions, each with four possible answers. You must choose the correct one.

Here are some of the things you will be tested on:

- The meanings of words
- The main idea of a passage
- What happens in a story
- Why an author wrote a passage
- Comparing two or more things
- Cause and effect
- Using materials to find information

Getting Ready for Test Day

The following is a list of things that can help you get ready for a test.

- Read at least thirty minutes per day.
- Practice reading different kinds of materials (newspapers, magazines, novels, stories, poetry, etc.).
- Set a daily time for studying and doing your homework.
- Set up a place to do your homework every day. Make sure it is quiet and well lit.
- Practice answering each kind of question that will be on the test.
- Review simple test-taking hints.
- Practice timed tests.
- Get enough sleep the night before the test.
- Eat a good breakfast on the day of the test.

What to Expect During a Test

The *Milestones* program will help you acquire and master the skills you will need to succeed in English. It will aid your progress in the following four skills: listening, speaking, reading, and writing.

You are about to take an assessment practice test. The purpose of the test is to measure your achievement in constructing meaning from a wide variety of texts. This practice includes many different kinds of reading passages followed by specific questions about the passages.

Each reading passage will be different. Some types of passages include factual articles, fictional stories, and poems. Always read the passages carefully. You can go back to a passage if you are not sure about something.

After reading each passage, you will then answer questions about the passages. Read the questions carefully. They will ask about parts of the passages such as facts, plot, or language.

On the actual test, you may also be given a map, chart, or picture. For those, you will have to read the titles and labels to answer the questions.

Your teacher will give you sample directions and questions before the test begins. Ask about anything you do not understand. Once the test begins, you will not be able to ask questions.

The test questions all have multiple-choice answers. A multiple-choice test item may ask you to answer a specific question, or it may ask you to complete a sentence. There will be four possible answers. Only one of them is correct. Read all of the choices carefully and choose the answer you think is correct. Don't spend too much time on one question. It is important to answer all of the questions on the test.

How to Read Questions

The following is a sample passage. Read the passage and then read the questions below.

Every morning, Isabella and her mother walk together to school. Isabella's mother always smiles and says, "Isabella, be careful when you cross the street." Her smile is gentle like a flower.

1 **Read this sentence from the passage.**

> Be careful when you cross the street.

What does _careful_ mean in this sentence?

A cautious

B bored

C happy

D tired

2 **Which word best tells about Isabella's mother's attitude toward Isabella?**

A patient

B clever

C nervous

D understanding

You will be asked to use a number two pencil on the test. Be sure to mark the correct answer on the answer sheet. Make sure the number on the answer sheet matches the number of the question. It is easy to make a mistake. If you do, your answers will be marked as wrong because they are in the wrong place. Don't change an answer unless you are sure that it is wrong. If you must change an answer, check the number and change the right one. Make sure that you answer every question. Do not leave any answers blank.

How to Answer Questions

When answering multiple-choice questions, read each answer carefully.

3   **Read this sentence from the passage.**

> Her smile is gentle like a flower.

What kind of sentence is this?

A   simile

B   metaphor

C   onomatopoeia

D   personification

If you come across an item that you do not know the answer to, here is one strategy you can use.

You might say: *There aren't any sounds in the sentence, so it is not onomatopoeia. There is no comparison to a person, so it is not personification. There is a comparison of one thing to another thing in this sentence, so it could be a metaphor. However, the word "like" is used, so it must be a simile. Therefore, the correct answer is letter a. This question is number 3. I will look at my answer sheet, find number 3, and mark letter a.*

The following pages contain a sample test. Read each passage carefully. Then use the answer sheet on page 5 to mark your answers.

Answer the questions that appear in the Assessment Practice Test on this Answer Sheet.

1	Ⓐ Ⓑ Ⓒ Ⓓ	27 Ⓐ Ⓑ Ⓒ Ⓓ	53 Ⓐ Ⓑ Ⓒ Ⓓ
2	Ⓐ Ⓑ Ⓒ Ⓓ	28 Ⓐ Ⓑ Ⓒ Ⓓ	54 Ⓐ Ⓑ Ⓒ Ⓓ
3	Ⓐ Ⓑ Ⓒ Ⓓ	29 Ⓐ Ⓑ Ⓒ Ⓓ	55 Ⓐ Ⓑ Ⓒ Ⓓ
4	Ⓐ Ⓑ Ⓒ Ⓓ	30 Ⓐ Ⓑ Ⓒ Ⓓ	56 Ⓐ Ⓑ Ⓒ Ⓓ
5	Ⓐ Ⓑ Ⓒ Ⓓ	31 Ⓐ Ⓑ Ⓒ Ⓓ	57 Ⓐ Ⓑ Ⓒ Ⓓ
6	Ⓐ Ⓑ Ⓒ Ⓓ	32 Ⓐ Ⓑ Ⓒ Ⓓ	58 Ⓐ Ⓑ Ⓒ Ⓓ
7	Ⓐ Ⓑ Ⓒ Ⓓ	33 Ⓐ Ⓑ Ⓒ Ⓓ	59 Ⓐ Ⓑ Ⓒ Ⓓ
8	Ⓐ Ⓑ Ⓒ Ⓓ	34 Ⓐ Ⓑ Ⓒ Ⓓ	60 Ⓐ Ⓑ Ⓒ Ⓓ
9	Ⓐ Ⓑ Ⓒ Ⓓ	35 Ⓐ Ⓑ Ⓒ Ⓓ	61 Ⓐ Ⓑ Ⓒ Ⓓ
10	Ⓐ Ⓑ Ⓒ Ⓓ	36 Ⓐ Ⓑ Ⓒ Ⓓ	62 Ⓐ Ⓑ Ⓒ Ⓓ
11	Ⓐ Ⓑ Ⓒ Ⓓ	37 Ⓐ Ⓑ Ⓒ Ⓓ	63 Ⓐ Ⓑ Ⓒ Ⓓ
12	Ⓐ Ⓑ Ⓒ Ⓓ	38 Ⓐ Ⓑ Ⓒ Ⓓ	64 Ⓐ Ⓑ Ⓒ Ⓓ
13	Ⓐ Ⓑ Ⓒ Ⓓ	39 Ⓐ Ⓑ Ⓒ Ⓓ	65 Ⓐ Ⓑ Ⓒ Ⓓ
14	Ⓐ Ⓑ Ⓒ Ⓓ	40 Ⓐ Ⓑ Ⓒ Ⓓ	
15	Ⓐ Ⓑ Ⓒ Ⓓ	41 Ⓐ Ⓑ Ⓒ Ⓓ	
16	Ⓐ Ⓑ Ⓒ Ⓓ	42 Ⓐ Ⓑ Ⓒ Ⓓ	
17	Ⓐ Ⓑ Ⓒ Ⓓ	43 Ⓐ Ⓑ Ⓒ Ⓓ	
18	Ⓐ Ⓑ Ⓒ Ⓓ	44 Ⓐ Ⓑ Ⓒ Ⓓ	
19	Ⓐ Ⓑ Ⓒ Ⓓ	45 Ⓐ Ⓑ Ⓒ Ⓓ	
20	Ⓐ Ⓑ Ⓒ Ⓓ	46 Ⓐ Ⓑ Ⓒ Ⓓ	
21	Ⓐ Ⓑ Ⓒ Ⓓ	47 Ⓐ Ⓑ Ⓒ Ⓓ	
22	Ⓐ Ⓑ Ⓒ Ⓓ	48 Ⓐ Ⓑ Ⓒ Ⓓ	
23	Ⓐ Ⓑ Ⓒ Ⓓ	49 Ⓐ Ⓑ Ⓒ Ⓓ	
24	Ⓐ Ⓑ Ⓒ Ⓓ	50 Ⓐ Ⓑ Ⓒ Ⓓ	
25	Ⓐ Ⓑ Ⓒ Ⓓ	51 Ⓐ Ⓑ Ⓒ Ⓓ	
26	Ⓐ Ⓑ Ⓒ Ⓓ	52 Ⓐ Ⓑ Ⓒ Ⓓ	

The Magic Coin Purse
A Folktale from Korea

1   There was a young couple who lived in a small cottage. They were poor, and every morning they chopped firewood. They chopped two bundles, one to light their own fire and one to trade for rice.

2   One day the extra bundle disappeared. The next day, it disappeared again. The man and woman were upset because they needed to sell the firewood to buy rice. On the third day, the husband hid himself in the bundle of wood. After a little while, he saw a giant rope come down from the sky and wrap around the bundle. It lifted the bundle all the way into the clouds.

3   When the bundle arrived above the clouds, the young woodcutter saw an old man. The old man untied the bundle of wood and laughed when he saw the woodcutter. "Why do you chop two bundles of wood?" the old man asked. "Most people only chop one."

4   The woodcutter answered, "My wife and I have very little money. We chop an extra bundle to sell for food."

5   The old man nodded. "I will give you a treasure from my kingdom." He gave the woodcutter a small coin purse. "This is empty, but if you reach into it once a day, you will pull out a silver coin. This will help you buy food. But remember, you can only pull out one coin a day."

6   The woodcutter thanked the old man for the gift. He took the coin purse and climbed back down the giant rope. The woodcutter explained everything to his wife. They agreed to save the money from the purse, but they could not agree what to buy.

7   The man wanted to buy an ox. The woman wanted to buy a goat. Finally, they agreed to buy land. They bought a few acres of good land and were satisfied. Then they wanted to build a brick house. The couple spent most of their money on bricks and other supplies. It was also costly to pay the carpenters and masons.

8   Finally the couple decided to take more money from the purse. They reached into the purse a second time on one day. When they received a second silver coin, they were overjoyed. They reached in a third time and found a third coin. The fourth time they reached in, the purse was empty. When they turned to look at the brick house, it had turned into their old cottage.

9   The couple laughed. "I guess we can't depend on coin purses from heaven. Let's go back to cutting wood."

If You Follow Trouble, Trouble Follows You
A Folktale from Ghana

1   Anansi was a spider. One day, he walked through the forest and saw some beautiful flowers. Then, King Tiger walked by and said, "Those are beautiful flowers. I shall call them Tiger Lilies."

2   He asked if King Tiger could name something after him. Tiger laughed. "You are so small," Tiger said. Then he thought and said, "OK. If you can tie up Snake and bring him to me, I will name something after you."

3   Everyone was afraid of Snake, even Tiger. Anansi thought for a long time about what to do. He thought of a clever plan. He decided to wait. Soon Snake heard about what Tiger and Anansi talked about. He laughed at first. But soon he got bored. Finally he went to Anansi's house.

4   "I know Tiger asked you to catch me," Snake said. "But I decided to come to you first. So here I am. Catch me now."

5   Anansi said, "I know I can't catch you. I wanted to tell Tiger how long you are and explain it is impossible. I was trying to figure out how to measure you. The only thing that's long enough is that piece of bamboo over there."

6   Snake laughed, "Don't you have eyes? I'm longer than the bamboo." Anansi agreed and said, "Maybe if I cut a piece down, I could measure you and see exactly how long you are."

7   Snake agreed. Anansi cut down the bamboo and put it next to Snake. The piece of bamboo was longer than Snake, which made Snake angry. Anansi said, "Maybe if I tie your tail to the end, you can stretch, and we'll see that you're longer than the bamboo." Snake agreed. Anansi tied his tail, but the bamboo was still longer.

8   "Maybe I should tie your middle to help you stretch?" Anansi asked. Snake wanted to show everyone how big he was, so he agreed. He kept stretching, but was still too short for the bamboo.

9   "I don't know what we can do," Anansi said. "Maybe we can tie your head," he said finally. "That will prove you are longer than the bamboo."

10   Snake nodded, and Anansi tied his head to the bamboo. Now Snake was longer. "OK, Anansi," Snake said. "You can untie me now. I'm longer than the bamboo."

11   "Let me go get my measuring tape," Anansi said. Anansi went and got Tiger. When everyone saw Snake tied to the bamboo, Tiger had to name something after Anansi. So he named the stories after him, which he called Anansi Stories.

1 What is the theme of "The Magic Coin Purse"?

A Always work hard.

B Don't be greedy.

C Don't build a brick house.

D Never trust strangers.

2 What did the old man do?

A Let the couple keep the brick house.

B Sent the couple extra bundles of wood.

C Gave the couple a rule to follow.

D Helped them decide what to buy.

3 Why was the couple upset about the missing bundle of firewood?

A They promised it to a friend.

B They used it to warm their house.

C They wanted to trade it for a small purse.

D They needed it to buy food.

4 What is an antonym for <u>overjoyed</u> (paragraph 8)?

A unhappy

B thrilled

C alarmed

D confused

5 Read this sentence from the story.

> They bought a few <u>acres</u> of good land and were satisfied.

What is the meaning of <u>acres</u> in this sentence?

A prices of land

B units of area

C brick houses

D costs of materials

6 What will the couple probably do next?

A ask the old man for another coin purse

B try to build another brick house

C ask the workers for their money back

D start selling bundles of wood again

7 In "If You Follow Trouble, Trouble Follows You," which word *best* describes Anansi?

A foolish

B ashamed

C clever

D crazy

8 Why did Tiger ask Anansi to tie up the Snake?

A He wanted to cause trouble for snakes.

B He didn't think Anansi could do it.

C He wanted people to make fun of Anansi.

D He thought it was an easy thing to do.

9 How will Snake probably treat Anansi in the future?

A He will treat him with respect.

B He will make fun of him.

C He will be his best friend.

D He will name other things after him.

10 Read this sentence from the story.

> Still, Anansi was <u>troubled</u> that everything was named after Tiger.

What does <u>troubled</u> mean in the sentence?

A made an effort

B faced with a problem

C worried about

D bothered by

11 What is *similar* in both stories?

A One character plays a trick on another.

B The story ends the way it begins.

C Both stories take place in an area near trees.

D A character is given a gift for his hard work.

12 How are the endings of these stories *alike*?

A A person did what they said they would do.

B Someone did not keep their promise.

C A character did not do what he set out to do.

D The main character is disappointed by the way things turn out.

How to Make a Paper Lantern

Introduction:

Paper lanterns are popular decorations for festivals like Chinese New Year. They are colorful and easy to make. They can be hung up around the house as holiday decorations.

What You Will Need:

- A sheet of colored paper
- Scissors
- Ruler
- Pencil
- Glue
- Paper clips
- Paint or stickers for decoration

What to Do:

Step 1   Fold a piece of paper in half the long way. Run your finger along the folded edge to fold it.

Step 2   Use a ruler and a pencil to mark the folded edge. Start from the left side and make a light pencil mark every inch.

Step 3   Cut slits in the folded paper using scissors. Cut one slit on each inch mark. Start cutting at the folded edge and stop one inch from the opposite edge.

Step 4   Unfold the paper and glue the short edges together. Use paper clips to hold the edges together while the glue dries.

Step 5   Make a handle for your lantern by cutting a strip of paper one inch wide. Glue the handle to each side of the top.

Step 6   Decorate your lantern with paint or stickers. You can also make your own designs using colored pens or pencils.

After You Have Finished:

Now that you know how to make one lantern, you can make more in different colors. Ask an adult to help you hang them up on a string.

How to Make Your Own Kazoo

Introduction:

A kazoo is a fun musical instrument. It buzzes when you hum through it. You can make one out of simple household items.

What You Will Need:

A cardboard tube   Glue
Waxed paper   Decorations (such as glitter, pens, or magic markers)
A ruler

What to Do:

Step 1   Measure the end of your cardboard tube.

Step 2   Cut out a square of waxed paper that is one inch larger than the end of the tube.

Step 3   Ask an adult to punch a hole in the middle of the tube. This will help air escape.

Step 4   Glue the waxed paper to the end of the tube. Make sure the waxed paper is attached tightly.

Step 5   Decorate your kazoo with glitter, pens, magic markers, or anything else.

Step 6   Hum through the end of the kazoo.

After You Have Finished:

Each kazoo will sound different. Make kazoos with your friends for a kazoo contest or play together as a kazoo chorus. Don't forget to tell your listeners that the kazoo is over 300 years old.

Tornadoes

1   Tornadoes are columns of air turning at high speeds. Tornadoes can occur at any time and place, but are most common in the United States in the Great Plains region during spring and summer.

2   Tornadoes often develop from strong thunderstorms. Thunderstorms happen when warm and moist air hits colder air. These storms produce lightning, thunder, hail, and strong winds. Before a thunderstorm happens, the direction of the wind and its speed change. This causes the air on the ground to spin.

3   Most tornadoes are weak tornadoes with winds less than 110 miles per hour. They last between one minute and ten minutes. Some tornadoes are strong tornadoes with winds up to 205 miles per hour. They last about 20 minutes. Two percent of all tornadoes are violent tornadoes with winds over 205 miles per hour. They last over an hour. They are the most dangerous tornadoes.

The American Badger

1   There are many varieties of badger. The American Badger is one type. All badgers have the same general characteristics. They are all short, squat with strong legs, and they are fantastic diggers. They have large front claws and two black stripes on their faces. The American badger also has two black marks on its cheeks. Its coat is silvery and thick.

2   All badgers like to make their homes underground. Eurasian badgers live in large systems of underground tunnels. American badgers dig different homes. They make simple dens in the area that they live in. They travel around and often dig new homes. In the winter, they stick close to one den and sleep a lot.

3   If a badger is threatened by a predator, it will walk backwards into its den. It keeps its teeth and claws out. Then it closes up the entrance to the den so the predator can't get in.

4   American badgers grow up to 30 inches long. Males average 19 pounds and females 15 pounds. Badgers in the wild usually live between eight and ten years. The oldest badger living in captivity was 26.

5   The main difference between the American badger and other badgers is diet. The American badger is an active hunter. It eats small mammals like squirrels, rats, gophers, and mice. It also eats insects, snakes, frogs, vegetables, and grains.

6   The hunting style of American badgers is also unusual. American badgers do not run after the animals they hunt. Instead, they dig down at great speeds to catch their dinner.

7   American badgers hide in their dens when they are threatened. They also fight off threats by hissing, growling, snarling, and squeaking. They can bite with powerful jaws and produce unpleasant smells. Their thick, loose fur helps protect them from predators. Badgers are hunted by bears, coyotes, cougars, and eagles.

8   American badgers usually hunt by night. In some areas they also hunt in the day. They live alone and do not like other badgers coming into their territory. American badgers like open areas like farmlands. They can be found in the United States from the West Coast to Ohio. They are also found in southern Canada and in Mexico.

13 In "How to Make a Paper Lantern," why do you need paper clips?

A to hold the edges together

B to hang the paper lantern

C to decorate the paper lantern

D to make the sharp crease

14 In "How to Make Your Own Kazoo," why do you need to punch a hole into the tube?

A so you can hum into the kazoo

B to help the air escape

C so you can attach the waxed paper

D to make the kazoo sound better

15 What are these two passages mostly about?

A things to make with household items

B learning the history of kazoos

C how to decorate a kazoo

D making an instrument

16 What is probably true about kazoos?

A Each kazoo may have a different sound.

B Kazoos are difficult to play.

C Only children should make them.

D Decorations affect the sound of the kazoo.

17 What is *similar* about these passages?

A You need waxed paper for both of them.

B They are both fun to play with.

C You may need an adult to help you.

D Both items should be hung on a string.

18 Why did the author write these passages?

A to give directions

B to tell a story

C to make you laugh

D to try to change your mind

19 Read this sentence from the passage, "Tornadoes."

> These storms <u>produce</u> lightning, thunder, hail, and strong winds.

What is the meaning of **produce**?

A to destroy

B to control

C to stop

D to create

20 How is a tornado *different* from a thunderstorm?

A It can happen anywhere.

B It can cause damage.

C It has stronger winds.

D It can happen at any time.

21 What causes air along the ground to spin?

A the direction of the wind and its speed change

B the lightning, thunder, and hail of a storm

C warm, moist air that collides with colder air

D the updraft pushing the air vertical

22 What type of storm has the strongest winds?

A a thunderstorm

B a violent tornado

C a strong tornado

D a weak tornado

23 What is this passage mostly about?

A places to find shelter

B learning tornado safety

C damage caused by weather

D a dangerous type of storm

24 **How do badgers get their food?**

A   They climb trees.

B   They hunt in open fields.

C   They dig into the ground.

D   They fish in streams.

25 **Why would a badger walk backwards into its den?**

A   It is looking for food.

B   A predator is after him.

C   It is protecting its babies.

D   Another badger is nearby.

26 **How are American badgers *different* from Eurasian badgers?**

A   They have strong legs.

B   They dig different homes.

C   They have facial markings.

D   They are great diggers.

27 **Why did the author write these passages?**

A   to persuade

B   to explain

C   to entertain

D   to inform

28 **What are *both* of these passages about?**

A   art

B   history

C   science

D   current events

Estuaries

1   An estuary is a place where rivers and oceans meet. Rivers have fresh water and oceans have salt water. In an estuary, the salt water and fresh water mix together. This creates important places for many kinds of birds, animals, and plants to live. The estuaries are sometimes the only place they can survive.

2   There are many kinds of estuaries. They have names like bays, harbors, or sounds. San Francisco Bay is an estuary. Puget Sound in Washington is an estuary. Chesapeake Bay in Maryland is an estuary. The New York and New Jersey Harbor is also an estuary.

3   Estuaries are important because of the many types of wildlife that live there. Some fish live in estuaries while they are young. Then they swim into the ocean when they are adults. This includes types of fish we buy in the supermarket.

4   Estuaries can also filter water. They make it cleaner for humans and wildlife. They protect the land from storms and floods. The plants in estuaries hold the land together so it does not wash away.

5   Since estuaries do so many things, it is important to protect them. There are a lot of beaches near estuaries. It is also popular to build houses on the coast. People build more new houses on the coast than in other areas. This means that the estuaries are in danger from pollution, new buildings, and human traffic. This can cause drinking water to become dangerous and fish to die. It is better for humans, animals, fish, birds, and plants to keep the estuaries clean.

Earth Day

1   Earth Day is a holiday to celebrate the Earth. The first Earth Day was in 1970. Twenty million people celebrated the first Earth Day in America. They wanted to help protect the Earth.

2   The first Earth Day got a lot of attention. People in the U.S. began to think about the environment. New laws were made to clean the air and water. Soon other laws were made to stop pollution and protect animals.

3   There are actually two Earth Days. There is an American Earth Day, which happens each year on April 22. There is also an international Earth Day, which happens each year on the first day of spring.

4   Earth Day is a holiday for the whole world. Hundreds of millions of people celebrate it each year. There are many ways to celebrate Earth Day. You can recycle. You can talk about the environment. You can also learn more about helping the planet.

29 What is "Estuaries" mostly about?

A   how pollution affects estuaries

B   where estuaries are located

C   what are the kinds of estuaries

D   why estuaries are important

30 Read this sentence from the passage.

> An estuary is a place where rivers and oceans **meet**.

What is the meaning of **meet** in this sentence?

A   get to know

B   come together

C   satisfy

D   struggle against

31 How do estuaries affect the land?

A   They wash away the soil.

B   They stir up damaging winds.

C   They protect the land from floods.

D   They cause violent storms.

32 Why was Earth Day first celebrated?

A   to start a new agency

B   to enjoy a beautiful day

C   to protect our environment

D   to begin an international holiday

33 What is a *similar* theme in these two passages?

A   Stand up for what you believe in.

B   Working together helps get things done.

C   Only worry about yourself.

D   Take care of the environment.

34 What do *both* of these passages talk about?

A   supplying food for the poor

B   protecting our wildlife

C   passing laws for clean air

D   caring for the world's children

A History of Radio

1   Radio is a way to send information through the air with waves. Radio waves are invisible. However, they can carry speech, music, and other sound. You can listen to the radio because of radio waves. Cordless phones and wireless computers also use radio waves.

2   Scientists discovered radio waves in the 1800s. A man named Guglielmo Marconi built the first machine to send and receive radio waves. It was called a wireless transmitter. Everyone sees Marconi as the father of the radio. He had many patents for his radio. Patents are proof that a new idea is yours. They allow you to control the use of an idea and make money from it.

3   Now people think that Marconi used someone else's ideas. There was another person who built radios at the same time. This person didn't want to control his ideas. He wanted people to use his ideas to improve the world. His name was Jagadish Chandra Bose.

4   Bose came from a part of India called Bengal. His first language was Bengali. He also spoke English. He went to university in England. Bose was a gifted scientist, naturalist, and author. He was good at many things.

5   After university, Bose returned to India and became a professor. He worked with radio waves. He wanted to use them to send messages. He also worked on the science of the waves. He was very clever at working with them. He published papers about his work in England.

6   Marconi read Bose's work. It helped him solve the problems with his wireless transmitter. Marconi was not a scientist. He didn't understand radio waves very well.

7   Marconi became famous. He did not give Bose credit for his work. Marconi's famous transmitter would not have been possible without it. Now, over 100 years later, the story of radio is clearer. Both Marconi and Bose are given credit for their work.

8   Today, we use radio waves in many ways. Mobile phones use radio waves to talk to each other. Astronauts use radio waves to talk to people on Earth. Doctors use radio waves to find illness. Even microwaves use radio waves to heat food. What a different world this would be without the work of Bose and Marconi!

Maria Mitchell, Astronomer

1   On August 1, 1818, a little girl was born. Her family lived on an island in Massachusetts called Nantucket. Her name was Maria Mitchell. She had a large family. She was number three of ten children.

2   Nantucket was a whaling island. Whaling ships set out from the harbors to travel on month-long trips looking for whales. They found their way across the ocean using the stars.

3   Someone who studies the stars is called an astronomer. Maria's father, William, was an astronomer. He was an expert in working with sextants. A sextant is a tool for measuring how high an object is in the sky. Sailors used sextants is to measure the height of the sun at noon. This helped them figure out where the ship was on the map.

4   William taught all of his children about the stars. He taught them to find groups of stars in the sky called constellations. He also taught them to see how the stars moved. Maria was the best. She learned most of what she knew by helping her father watch the stars at night.

5   Her father sent her to school to learn mathematics. He didn't have higher mathematical training. He wanted his daughter to have a better education. It was not common to give girls much education at that time. Maria was lucky to go to a school run by a man named Cyrus Peirce. Peirce believed in full education for girls. After two years, Maria was teaching at Peirce's school.

6   Maria became a librarian in 1836. She was eighteen years old. She read all of the books she could during the day and studied the stars at night. To watch the sky, she used a telescope. A telescope sees much further into the night sky than the naked eye.

7   On October 1, 1847, Maria Mitchell made an amazing discovery. With her telescope, she saw a new comet. There was a prize for people who found new comets with telescopes. The King of Denmark gave this prize. Maria Mitchell became the first American and the first woman to win the prize. The King of Denmark gave her a gold medal. This was a great honor. She was immediately famous.

8   The next year, Maria was the first woman to join the American Academy of Arts and Sciences. It is very hard to get into this group. Maria Mitchell was the first woman invited to join. She was also the only woman to join for one hundred years.

9   Maria became the first woman astronomer in America. She traveled all over the country and all over Europe. She taught astronomy at a college in New York called Vassar College. This was an important college for women. Maria taught many famous American women.

10   Maria Mitchell died in 1889. She was 70 years old. She had a long and successful career. Through learning and patient watching, she went from a quiet island to worldwide fame. She proved that women could be astronomers. Maria Mitchell reached for the stars. She taught other people to reach, too.

35 In "A History of Radio," what is the meaning of <u>invisible</u> (paragraph 1)?

A not able to be seen

B moving quickly

C without much effort

D a clear view

36 Why would someone want to get a patent?

A so that others can copy their invention

B to be in control of what you invented

C so that they can send and receive messages

D to be able to say things without proof

37 What is the message of this passage?

A Give credit where it is due.

B It is best to help one another.

C Inventions change the world.

D There are many ways to use things.

38 How are Marconi and Bose ALIKE?

A They both patented their invention.

B They were both gifted scientists.

C They both published papers about their work.

D They are both credited for their work today.

39 What will most likely happen?

A People will find more uses for radio waves.

B People will no longer get patents for their ideas.

C Other people will be credited for helping Marconi.

D People will be less interested in inventing new things.

40 In "Maria Mitchell, Astronomer," who *most* encouraged Maria to be an astronomer?

A   a teacher

B   her mother

C   her father

D   the king

41 What did Maria do FIRST?

A   She joined the American Academy of Arts and Sciences.

B   She won a prize for spotting a new comet.

C   She became the first professional woman astronomer.

D   She went to school to learn mathematics.

42 How might a sextant be useful to sailors?

A   It helps them find their location.

B   It helps them raise their sails.

C   It tells what direction they are going.

D   It tells the speed at which they are moving.

43 Why did Maria's father want her to learn mathematics?

A   He wanted her to have a better education than him.

B   He wanted her to become famous worldwide.

C   He wanted her to receive the gold medal from the king.

D   He wanted her to teach astronomy at Vassar College.

44 What is a common theme in these passages?

A   Parents want the best for their children.

B   Do not give up when things get difficult.

C   We should recognize people who help us.

D   Talented people have an effect on others.

45 How are these two passages *alike*?

A   They are both about famous scientists.

B   They are both about the struggle of women.

C   They are both about inventing new things.

D   They are both about having the support of family.

Hiram Bingham and the Lost City of Machu Picchu

1   Hiram Bingham had been walking for days. The cold mountains of Peru were tall and dangerous. He had to continue. He was looking for the legendary Inca mountain capital.

2   Hiram had heard many stories of the capital. He paid a guide to lead him six days out of the nearest town and far up into the mountains. The path was very steep. Hiram walked carefully to avoid falling. They climbed for days and days.

3   They finally reached the top at about 8,000 feet above sea level. In front of Hiram lay the most amazing ruins he had ever seen. Beautiful stone walls and grassy paths were nestled inside the swift-moving Urubamba River.

4   There were many buildings connected by paths and stairs. There were also water fountains and streams. All of it was carved from rock.

5   Hiram wrote down everything he saw. He wanted to collect as much information as possible. He wanted to tell the world about Machu Picchu.

6   Machu Picchu is now a very important archeological site. It is also a very popular tourist destination. Many people study Machu Picchu, but it is still a mystery why and how the city was built.

7   Of course, Machu Picchu was never truly lost. The people who lived nearby always knew about it. However, Hiram Bingham brought Machu Picchu to the attention of the world.

Hmong Vegetable Story

1   Many years ago my family left their home country. They came from Laos in Asia. My grandparents and their family left because of a war. They didn't have much money, but many nice people helped them along the way.

2   One day my grandmother came home with good news. She found a place to make a garden. She missed the vegetables of Laos. American vegetables were very different and very expensive.

3   My grandmother rented land from a nearby farmer. She started with cucumbers and squash. She was very successful. Soon, my grandmother's friends joined her. They began to work together in their gardens. They wanted to help each other so everyone could grow vegetables for their families.

4   They were so successful that soon they had extra vegetables to sell to other people. Some of the vegetables they grew were very unusual. Everyone was interested. The stores in the area heard about the vegetables. So did some of the restaurants.

5   Now they sell their vegetables to everyone. It is a very good business. My grandmother likes to work with the soil. She loves growing fresh food for our family. She even taught me how to have a garden. When I grow up, I hope I can feed my family with fresh vegetables too.

46 Why is Machu Picchu a mystery?

A   No one wants to study it.

B   We don't know why it was built.

C   No one ever lived in the area.

D   People do not want to visit it.

47 What was Hiram Bingham looking for?

A   the Inca mountain capital

B   stone water fountains

C   the Urubamba River

D   a mountain-climbing guide

48 What is the passage mostly about?

A   people living in a city in the mountains

B   how to make a city out of stone

C   a man discovering an important site

D   what people like best about the Lost City

49 In the "Hmong Vegetable Story," what is true about the grandmother's friends?

A   They are unhappy in America.

B   They want to keep all of the vegetables.

C   They help each other with their gardens.

D   They only grew American vegetables.

50 Why did the grandmother want to plant a garden?

A   She needed something to do with her time.

B   Their home had a yard with space for a guide.

C   American vegetables cost too much.

D   She wanted to work with her friends.

51 What do *both* of these passages have in common?

A   friends who help each other

B   someone who collects information

C   a place that people like to visit

D   characters who traveled

The Story of San Juan Capistrano

1   The swallows return to San Juan Capistrano every March. They fly back from their winter home in Argentina. They come back each year at the same time. They have seen many changes over the years.

2   First, the Acjachemen people lived there in small houses by the coast. Their ancestors had lived there for thousands of years. They had a close relationship with the ocean. They lived on the land in small groups.

3   In 1769 the Spanish came. The Spanish government was interested in the new land of California. They sent a man named Junipero Serra. He built missions to bring a new style of life to the area. This style of life was working together on a common farm and living together in larger houses. There were also military forts called presidios near the missions. These forts helped the army protect the people living on the missions.

4   The Spanish government wanted to protect California from other countries. The Russian government was on the coast above California. The Spanish government didn't want the Russians to take away California.

5   Together, the army and the missions expanded. The Spanish built 21 missions from San Diego in the south to San Francisco in the north. It took one day to ride with a horse from mission to mission. It took three days walking. The distance between the missions was about 30 miles.

6   At San Juan Capistrano, the Spanish took people from their tribes. They wanted them to live in the mission buildings. Inside, the Acjachemen people saw many new things. The Spanish brought many tools from home. The Spanish also brought living things from Spain. Among these were sheep, mules, horses, and fruit trees.

7   In the years that followed, the Acjachemen and the Spanish lived together. It was not easy. Many of the Acjachemen died from diseases that came from Europe. Also, if people went to the mission they had to leave their families. This separated a lot of people. The rules were strict at the mission and the work was hard.

8   San Juan Capistrano was founded in 1776. This was the year of the American Declaration of Independence. Many things have changed, but many things remain. The families of the Acjachemen still live in San Juan Capistrano. The mission still stands and is in use. The swallows come back every year.

52 What is the meaning of <u>expanded</u> (paragraph 5)?

   A   opened wide

   B   increased in number

   C   moved away

   D   separated

53 What was a problem for the Acjachemen people?

   A   They had to fight against the Russian soldiers.

   B   They were no longer able to see the swallows.

   C   They had to move their families to San Francisco.

   D   They died from diseases that came from Europe.

54 What happened *first*?

   A   San Juan Capistrano was founded by the Spanish.

   B   The Spanish built 21 missions in California.

   C   The Acjachemen people lived by the coast.

   D   The Spanish took people to live in the mission buildings.

55 Why did the Spanish build forts?

   A   to protect the area from other countries

   B   to keep the Acjachemen out of the missions

   C   to have a place for the missionaries to live

   D   to house the animals they brought from Spain

56 How did life change for the Acjachemen people?

   A   It was better than before.

   B   It stayed about the same.

   C   It became more difficult.

   D   It was what they hoped for.

Alien Dog

1   My dog can change TV channels by waggling his ears. He can also predict the weather. As you may guess, my dog is no ordinary dog. He's an alien.

2   It started on a cold and rainy night. We were driving home from my friend James's house. My mom was listening to the radio. Suddenly, it didn't sound normal. The radio started to crackle, pop, and screech.

3   In a nearby field, there was a bright blue light and a loud boom. The car shook. Something had fallen through the trees at the end of the field. I could see it glowing from our car.

4   I was a little scared. I didn't know what was happening. My mom wanted to make sure everyone was okay. She thought maybe it was a plane or a helicopter and people were hurt.

5   We called my aunt to tell her what we were doing. Then we went up to the field together. There, in the field, near the trees, there was a large hole. There was a glowing substance in the hole. Out of the trees came Flip, my dog.

6   He was so cute. He was black and furry and the size of a large poodle. He was also very friendly. We could tell he was hungry, so we fed him salami and water from the car. Somehow everything wasn't scary when Flip was with us.

7   Mom looked around but she couldn't see anything. There wasn't a plane or a helicopter. Finally, we got in the car and went back home. At first, Mom didn't want to take Flip. She was worried that he belonged to a family in the area. However, there weren't any houses nearby, so she agreed.

8   She was still worried that people were looking for Flip. We put up "found dog" posters but nobody came to get him. I was really happy. I liked playing with Flip. He was good at catching. He almost seemed to float in the air while he did it.

9   One day, I discovered him going in and out of the house. I didn't know dogs could use doorknobs. Another day I was watching TV. I was watching a nature show called "Wolftown." It was good, but I wanted to watch a cartoon instead. I switched the channel with the remote control. Flip stood up. He waggled his ears, and the TV went back to "Wolftown." Amazed, I changed the channel back to my cartoon. Then he did it again. Since then, we have made a compromise. Sometimes we watch nature shows. Sometimes we watch cartoons.

10   Flip always brings me an umbrella if it is raining. He's also becoming good at opening the refrigerator. Mom and I have agreed not to tell anyone else about Flip's special abilities. Sometimes I wonder if his people will come back and get him from Earth. Right now, he's pretty happy with the salami and the nature shows.

57 Read this sentence from the passage, "Alien Dog."

> Since then, we have made a compromise.

What does <u>compromise</u> mean?

A   wanting your own way

B   settling of differences

C   watching a favorite program

D   trying something different

58 Why did they put up a poster?

A   to get another dog

B   to see the dog

C   to give the dog away

D   to find the dog's owner

59 What word *best* describes the dog?

A   foolish

B   ordinary

C   dangerous

D   unusual

60 Where did this dog come from?

A   out of the trees

B   from a helicopter

C   from a plane

D   out of the hole

61 Why did Mom agree to keep Flip?

A   because he was such a cute dog

B   because she didn't know who he belonged to

C   because she wanted to make her children happy

D   because she knew he could do tricks

Read the following entries from a thesaurus. Then answer the questions.

brave (adj.)

1. bold, adventurous, daring

2. courageous, fearless

3. (slang) chin-up

brave (v.)

1. endure, bear

2. challenge, face

3. suffer

4. (ant.) break down, give up, run away

62 Which word entry gives a slang form?

A   courageous (adj.)

B   brave (adj.)

C   brave (v.)

D   face (v.)

63 Which word could be listed as an ANTONYM for the adjective brave?

A   unafraid

B   oppose

C   cowardly

D   encounter

64 We will go out and brave the cold weather.

Which entry for brave (v.) BEST replaces it in this sentence?

A   1

B   2

C   3

D   4

65 What part of speech is brave when it means suffer?

A   verb

B   adverb

C   noun

D   adjective

Name _____ Date _____

● Vocabulary From the Reading

Use with student book page 6.

> **Key Vocabulary**
>
> annoyed   traditional
> scare   wise
> surprised

A.   Circle the correct word in each sentence.

Example: Tamales are a (wise / (traditional)) food in Mexico.

1.   We were (surprised / wise). We didn't expect to win the soccer game.

2.   Marta won't touch dogs. They (surprise / scare) her.

3.   The teacher answers all our questions. She is very (wise / surprised).

4.   My dog barked all night. My father was (annoyed / traditional).

B.   Match the underlined word to its definition.

Example: __e__ The rain during the soccer match <u>annoyed</u> us.

1.   _____ People who give good advice are <u>wise</u>.

2.   _____ Driving <u>scares</u> me. I am afraid of having an accident.

3.   _____ It is <u>traditional</u> for an American bride to wear a white dress.

4.   _____ I did not know you had a sister. I am <u>surprised</u>.

    a.   usual, normal

    b.   causes fear

    c.   amazed by something someone didn't expect

    d.   smart, intelligent

    e.   ~~caused a little anger~~

C.   Write sentences. Use one of the Key Vocabulary words in each sentence.

Example: _I was surprised to see my mother ride a bicycle._

1.   _____

2.   _____

3.   _____

4.   _____

Name _____ Date _____

● Reading Strategy
Visualize

Use with student book page 7.

> When you **visualize,** you make an **image** of something in your mind.

Academic Vocabulary for the Reading Strategy	
Word	**Explanation**
visualize	to make a picture in your mind
image	a picture you make in your mind

Read the passage. Then complete the chart. Use examples from the passage.

1. I love to buy new clothes, and the Brentwood Mall is my favorite place to shop. I always have a good time there. There are rows of tall palm trees all around the mall. They look really nice. We park near the main entrance. Then we go in through these big glass doors. Cool air hits me in the face. It feels great!

2. It's never quiet inside the mall. The first thing we see is the children's merry-go-round. The horses look like they're jumping up and down. There are also life-size elephants and giraffes. The singsong music of the merry-go-round mixes with children's laughter.

3. We pass the taco stand. I smell the onions and grilled meat. I decide to have one later. But now it's time to shop. We stop at a T-shirt store with a display of red, orange, and yellow shirts. I buy two. Then we decide to go back to the taco stand. We sit and enjoy our tacos and listen to lively Mexican music. I love a spicy, hot taco with a glass of ice-cold tea!

see	hear	taste	smell	feel
tall palm trees				

Milestones A • Copyright © Heinle

Name _____ Date _____

● **Text Genre**
Short Story

Use with student book page 8.

Short Story	
characters	people in a story
setting	where the story happens
plot	events in a story that happen in a certain order
theme	the meaning or message of the story

Read the story. Then label the sentences listed below it. Use the words **character, setting, plot,** or **theme.**

(1) Gloria and her friend Iris are shopping at the Goodrich Shopping Center. (2) The mall is full of people and there are "Sale" signs on all the walls. (3) Gloria is smiling and laughing. (4) She's very excited. (5) Her uncle gave her $25. (6) She's planning to buy a pair of gold earrings. (7) Iris tells Gloria that she only has $5 to spend. (8) She looks tired and sad.

(9) The two girls stop to look at some earrings. (10) Suddenly Gloria stops looking at the earrings and looks at Iris. (11) Then she smiles and says to Iris, "I'm going to take you to the movies instead of buying earrings." (12) "But you really want them," says Iris. (13) "I can always get them another day," says Gloria. (14) And the two girls go off happily to the movies. (15) Sometimes friendship is more important than money.

Example: Sentence 2 _____setting_____

1. Sentences 3 and 4 _____

2. Sentences 5 and 6 _____

3. Sentence 8 _____

4. Sentences 9 and 10 _____

5. Sentence 15 _____

Name _____ Date _____

● Reading Comprehension

Use with student book page 15.

Academic Vocabulary for the Reading Comprehension Questions	
Word	**Explanation**
conclusion	a judgment or an opinion that you make from information you know
recognize	to remember someone or something when you see that person or thing

A. **Retell the story.** Tell the story "My Korean Name" in your own words. Include the main points of the plot. Tell what conclusion you can make about the grandfather. At the end, explain the theme of the story.

_____

_____

_____

_____

_____

_____

_____

B. **Write your response.** Won Chul changed by spending time with his grandfather. Does spending time with your relatives change you in any way? Can you recognize things in your relatives that you see in yourself? Explain.

_____

_____

_____

_____

C. **Assess the reading strategy.** Look back at the passage on page 30 in this book. Choose two senses. Describe how they help you visualize the reading.

_____

_____

_____

_____

Milestones A • Copyright © Heinle

Name _____ Date _____

● Literary Element

Use with student book page 15.

Characterization

> **Characterization** is how a writer shows what a character is like. Writers describe what the character looks like. They describe the character's words, thoughts, and actions. They show what other people think about the character.

A. Read the following two paragraphs. Then answer the questions.

My best friend's name is Ali. He came here last year from Turkey. At first, I thought he was unfriendly because he was so quiet. But then we became friends because we both love soccer a lot. Now I think he's really cool. We play on the school team. He's a forward and I'm a defender. Ali's really tall. He always wears a T-shirt with the name of his favorite team on the back.

One day after practice he invited me to visit his family. We were walking down the street. Ali seemed to be thinking. Suddenly he said, "You may think my family is a little strange. They aren't used to this country yet." "Don't worry," I told him. "My family has always lived here, and they're pretty weird, too." Ali looked at me and then laughed out loud.

1. How does Ali look? Copy two sentences here.

_____

_____

_____

2. What is Ali thinking? Copy one sentence here.

_____

_____

3. What does Ali do at the very end of the second paragraph? Copy one sentence here.

_____

_____

4. What does another person think about Ali? Copy one sentence here.

_____

_____

Name _____ Date _____

● Vocabulary From the Reading

Use with student book page 16.

Key Vocabulary

belong   tradition
role

A. Complete the chart. Write your own definitions. Add an example sentence for each item.

Word	Your Definition of the Word	Example Sentence
belong	to be the property of someone	The red bicycle belongs to me.
role		
tradition		

B. Complete each sentence. Use one of the Key Vocabulary words.

Example: My sisters _____ belong _____ to a dance club.

1. I always have chicken and rice on my birthday. It is a _____.

2. What _____ do you take with your friends? Are you a leader?

3. My family has a _____ of having pizza every Saturday.

4. Does that dog _____ to you?

C. Write a paragraph about someone you know. Use the three Key Vocabulary words in your paragraph.

_____

_____

_____

_____

_____

Name _____ Date _____

● Reading Strategy
Ask Questions

Use with student book page 17.

> If you **ask questions** as you read, you will focus on the reading better.

A. Read the following paragraphs.

Volcanoes are among nature's most dangerous forces. For many years, scientists have studied them. However, researchers still haven't predicted most volcanic eruptions. Almost every year, hundreds of people die because of volcanoes. Despite this, many thousands of people continue to live close to active volcanoes. Perhaps there is one near where you are living right now.

Scientists would like to monitor the volcanic activity of all volcanoes near where people live. However, setting up thousands of monitoring stations is just too expensive. It would cost millions of dollars to keep track of hundreds of volcanoes that will never erupt. However, since the beginning of history, people have chosen to live near volcanoes. This is because the soil there is very fertile. Crops grow beautifully in volcanic soil. Many very old cities started out this way and people just don't want to leave them.

B. Look back at the paragraphs above. Write a question starting with **Why** about each underlined sentence.

Question 1: _____

_____

Answer 1: _____

_____

Question 2: _____

_____

Answer 2: _____

_____

Name _____ Date _____

● **Text Genre**   *Use with student book page 17.*
Informational Text

Informational Text	
headings	titles of sections
facts	statements that are true
examples	something that shows or explains a fact

Read the informational text below. Then complete the chart.

National Parks in the U.S.

Today there are 391 national parks in the United States. The first one opened in 1864 in California. Sequoia and Kings Canyon Parks protect some very special things. For example, there are some very old giant sequoia trees. There are also some important American Indian historical sites.

National Parks in Europe

Europeans soon followed the example of the U.S. Today, Europe has over 350 national parks. The first one in France, Vanoise National Park, opened in 1963. The idea of a national park was first discussed in the 1940s. However, there were some problems. For example, people couldn't agree on the size the park should be. Also, they had different ideas about whether human or animal needs should come first. Today, the park serves the needs of both people and animals.

Feature	Examples from the Text
headings	• (Paragraph 1) _____ • (Paragraph 2) _____
facts	(Paragraph 1) • There are 391 national parks in the United States. _____ • _____ (Paragraph 2) • _____ • _____
examples	(Paragraph 1) • _____ • _____ (Paragraph 2) • _____ • _____

Name _____ Date _____

● Reading Comprehension

Use with student book page 21.

A. **Draw your own conclusions.** Write the most important information in "Home Life in Ancient Greece." Then write your conclusions about ancient Greece.

_____

_____

_____

_____

_____

_____

B. **Write your response.** Can you recognize the differences between life in ancient Greece and life in the United States today? What are they? Which way of life do you think is better? Why?

_____

_____

_____

_____

C. **Assess the reading strategy.** How does asking questions as you read improve your understanding of the text?

_____

_____

_____

_____

Name _____ Date _____

● Spelling

Use with student book page 21.

Words with the Same Sound but Different Spellings

The words **to, too,** and **two** have the same sound. When you write, be sure you use the correct spelling of each one.

Word	Meaning	Example
to	in the direction of	We go **to** the mall every week.
too	also; more than enough	I like math, and I like English, **too.** Close the window. It's **too** cold in here.
two	the number 2	I have **two** sisters.

A. Read the sentences and circle the correct word.

Example: I'm hungry! I want (to / too /(two)) slices of pizza.

1. I want to go (to / too / two) the soccer game on Saturday.

2. (To / Too / Two) students in my class are from Africa.

3. My family moved (to / too / two) the United States (to / too / two) years ago.

4. The math problem was (to / too / two) difficult for me

5. Magda likes Brazilian music, and I like it, (to / too / two).

6. It's 8:00! It's (to / too / two) early to go to bed!

B. Fill in the blanks with **to, too,** or **two.**

Every day, my (1) _____ brothers walk (2) _____ school with me. We go (3) _____ our classes. I have lunch with my (4) _____ friends, Carlos and Amy. I have fun, and they have fun, (5) _____. When I get home, I do my homework. I think I have (6) _____ much homework!

C. Write three sentences. Use the word in parentheses.

1. (to) _____

2. (too) _____

3. (two) _____

Name _____   Date _____

● **Writing Conventions**   *Use with student book page 21.*
  Spelling: Contractions

> When we combine words, we sometimes leave out a letter. This is called a
> **contraction.** An apostrophe (') shows where the letter or letters have been left out.
>
> | | | |
> |---|---|---|
> | I'm = I am | we're = we are | he's = he is |
> | you're = you are | she's = she is | they're = they are |

A. Rewrite these sentence. Use contractions.

Example: You are very tall. _You're very tall._ _____

1. I am a singer. _____

2. He is intelligent. _____

3. They are from Mexico. _____

4. You are a good soccer player. _____

  Punctuation: Parentheses

> **Parentheses** are used around words, phrases, or whole sentences. The words inside
> the parentheses add information or make an idea clearer.

B. Rewrite the sentences. Use a phrase from the box to make each sentence
      clearer. Put the phrase in parentheses.

~~particularly cats~~	my brother	like mine

Example: Some animals love fish.
     Some animals (particularly cats) love fish.

1. Bobby won his first race yesterday.

    _____

2. Some dogs are hard to train.

    _____

Name _____ Date _____

● Vocabulary Development

Use with student book page 23.

Suffixes: -y, -ful, -al

> The suffixes **-y, -ful,** and **-al** change nouns into adjectives.

A. Look at each word. Write the root word. Then write the suffix.

Adjective	Root Word (Noun)	Suffix
windy	wind	-y
1. powerful		
2. fictional		
3. meaningful		
4. national		
5. lucky		
6. rainy		
7. cheerful		
8. additional		

B. Complete each sentence with one of the adjectives above.

Example: The president is a very _____powerful_____ person.

1. Washington, D.C., is the _____ capital.

2. After two weeks, one _____ student joined the class.

3. It's a _____ day. Be sure to put on your raincoat.

4. Tom looks happy. He has a _____ look on his face.

5. We almost lost the game, but we were _____ at the end.

6. I saw a movie about my country. It was very _____ to me.

7. This story isn't true. It's _____.

8. We wanted to go swimming, but we weren't _____ because it

   was _____.

Name _____ Date _____

● Grammar

Use with student book page 24.

The Simple Present Tense of *be*

The Simple Present Tense of be		
subject	***be***	
I	**am**	
He / She / It	**is**	in class now.
You / We / They	**are**	

A. Circle the correct answer. Make sure the verb agrees with the subject.

Example: Yoko ((is)/ are) from Japan.

1. Anna and Carlos (am / are) from Mexico.

2. Linda (is / are) 15 years old.

3. I (am / are) in the classroom.

4. The children (is / are) at the movies.

5. You and I (is / are) cousins.

6. That desk (is / are) very old.

7. The students and the teacher (is / are) in the library.

8. I (is / am) the leader.

B. Complete these sentences. Use the simple present tense of **be.** Tell the truth.

Example: The weather ___is warm today_____

1. I _____

2. My family _____

3. My best friend _____

4. My friends and I _____

Name _____ Date _____

● Grammar

Use with student book page 25.

The Present Progressive Tense

Present Progressive Tense		
subject	be	verb + ing
I	am	
He / She / It	is	eating.
You / We / They	are	

A. Circle the correct answer.

Example: We (talking / (are talking)) about Korea.

1. Grandfather (live / is living) in the attic.

2. I (drinking / am drinking) tea with him.

3. He (am doing / is doing) calligraphy.

4. He and the boy (are talking / is talking).

5. You (are enjoying / are enjoy) that story.

B. Complete each sentence. Use the present progressive form of the verb in parentheses.

Example: They _____ are doing _____ (do) homework.

1. The boy _____ (make) tea for his grandfather.

2. Grandfather _____ (wear) a nice shirt.

3. They _____ (get) tired.

C. Tell what your friends and family members are doing right now. Use the present progressive tense.

Example: _____ Mario is sleeping. _____

1. _____

2. _____

3. _____

Milestones A • Copyright © Heinle

Name _____ Date _____

● Grammar Expansion
Yes/No Questions

Yes/No Questions with the Present Tense of *be*		
Present Tense of *be*	**Subject**	
Am	I	
Is	he / she / it	happy?
Are	you / we / they	

Yes/No Questions with the Present Progressive Tense		
Present Tense of *Be*	**Subject**	**Verb + *ing***
Am	I	
Is	he / she / it	working?
Are	you / we / they	

A. Unscramble the words and phrases to make questions.

Example: is / in his bedroom / Grandfather
___Is Grandfather in his bedroom?___

1. the boy / making / tea / is

   _____

2. are / from Korea / Won Chul's parents

   _____

3. I / am / a good calligraphy artist

   _____

B. Rewrite the sentences to make **yes/no** questions.

Example: You are doing your homework. ___Are you doing your homework?___

1. He is from Korea. _____

2. Grandfather is sleeping. _____

C. Write two **yes/no** questions about what a friend is doing now.

Example: ___Is Pablo doing his homework?___

1. _____

2. _____

43

Name _____ Date _____

● Grammar Expansion
Negative Statements

Negative Statements with the Present Tense of *be*		
Subject	*be* + *not*	
I	am **not**	
He / She / It	is **not**	happy.
You / We / They	are **not**	

Negative Statements with the Present Progressive Tense		
Subject	*be* + *not*	Verb + *ing*
I	am **not**	
He / She / It	is **not**	work*ing*?
You / We / They	are **not**	

A. Rewrite these sentences to make them negative.

Example: Won Chul's parents are from China.
  Won Chul's parents are not from China.

1. California is in Canada.

  _____

2. The students are singing a Mexican song.

  _____

3. My mother is making pizza for dinner.

  _____

4. I am at a soccer game now.

  _____

B. There are errors in these sentences. Rewrite them correctly.

Example: I not doing my homework. *I am not doing my homework.*

1. Maria is home not. _____

2. We watching not TV. _____

C. Write two negative sentences about yourself.

1. _____

2. _____

Name _____ Date _____

● Writing Assignment
Use with student book pages 26–27.

Descriptive Writing: Write a Paragraph About a Place

Fill in this chart to help you prewrite your descriptive paragraph.

Several places to write about	• *my grandmother's kitchen*
	•
	•
	•
	•
	•
Place I choose to write about	•
Things I visualize in this place	• Things I see:
	• Things I hear:
	• Things I smell or taste:
	• Things I feel:
Other information about this place	•
	•
	•

Name _____ Date _____

● Writing Assignment
Writing Support

Use with student book page 27.

Spelling: Singular and Plural Nouns

Put an **s** at the end of most singular nouns to make them plural.
    seagull / seagull**s**
For nouns that end in **s, x, ch,** or **sh,** add **es**.
    sandwich / sandwich**es**
For nouns that end in a consonant + **y**, change **y** to **i** and add **es**.
    family / famil**ies**
For nouns that end in **f** or **fe**, change the **f** or **fe** to **ves**.
    loaf / loa**ves**

A. Complete the sentences. Use the plural form of the words in the box.

dish	apple	knife	match	~~city~~	boy

Example: Chicago and Boston are big __*cities*__.

1. My _____ were wet. I couldn't start a fire.

2. My favorite fruits are oranges and _____.

3. There are ten girls and twelve _____ in my class.

4. I put the dirty _____ in the dishwasher.

5. I also put the _____, forks, and spoons in the dishwasher.

B. Write some sentences about places you have been. Use the plural form of one of the words in the box in each sentence.

monkey	lady	radio	leaf	~~house~~	beach	shelf	box

Example: __All the houses on this block are exactly the same.__

1. _____

2. _____

3. _____

Milestones A • Copyright © Heinle

Name _____ Date _____

● **Writing Assignment**
Revising Activity

Use with student book page 27.

Read each revision tip. Then rewrite the sentences in the charts to make them better.

Revision Tip # 1: Help the reader visualize what you are describing. Use adjectives and details.

First Try	A Better Way to Say It
Example: Angie's dress is red.	Angie's dress is the color of a ripe, red tomato.
1. (Seeing) The decorations are pretty.	
2. (Hearing) The music is loud.	
3. (Smelling) The food smells good.	
4. (Tasting) The cake tastes great.	
5. (Touching) The room is very hot.	

Revision Tip # 2: Use present progressive verbs for things happening now and to add lively details.

First Try	A Better Way to Say It
Example: There are dancers on the floor.	My uncle is dancing with my aunt. Little children are jumping up and down to the music.
1. There is good food to eat.	
2. Some older people sit and talk.	
3. A mother holds a little baby.	

Name _____ Date _____

● Writing Assignment

Use with student book page 27.

Editing Activity

Read the story and find the mistakes. Mark the mistakes using the editing marks on page 419 of your student book. Then rewrite the story correctly.

The school Library

A lot of kids is working in the library this morning. The librarian is talking to a group of boyes. they are looking for books about cars. The librarian is pointing to the shelfs under the window. She says there are some good car books there. Rita using a computer to do Internet research. She is writing a story about her favorite singer. she wants to find a picture of him online. Kenji is siting at a table all by himself. He is wearing glassis. He reading a book about soccer. Now the bell rings, and everyone runs out of the room.

_____

_____

_____

_____

_____

_____

_____

_____

_____

_____

_____

_____

Milestones A • Copyright © Heinle

Name _____ Date _____

● Vocabulary From the Reading

Use with student book page 32.

> **Key Vocabulary**
>
> ancestor   inheritance
> environment   lifestyle
> generation   personality

A. Read the clues. Use the Key Vocabulary words to complete the puzzle.

Across

2. group of people born at the same time period

4. something passed down from a relative

5. the air, land, and water around you

6. the way a person thinks, feels, and acts

Down

1. a parent, grandparent, etc.

3. the way a person lives

[crossword grid with 1. down spelling A N C E S T O R]

B. Choose one of the Key Vocabulary words. Tell why the idea behind this word is important to you. Give examples from your own life.

Example: ___We shouldn't forget our ancestors. My grandmother came to this___

___country alone at age 17. She became a teacher. She is a good example for me.___

_____

_____

_____

Name _____ Date _____

● Reading Strategy

Use with student book page 33.

Paraphrase

> When you **paraphrase** a **complex** sentence, you **simplify** it and put it in your own words.

Academic Vocabulary for the Reading Strategy	
Word	Explanation
complex	having many parts or details that make something hard to understand or work with
simplify	to make something less **complex** or less difficult to understand

Read the paragraph. Copy the underlined complex sentences under the heading *Sentence* in the chart. Then paraphrase the sentences to make them simpler.

Some students find algebra to be something that they could do without. They dislike doing long, complicated problems. However, Mrs. Clark thinks that she has the perfect solution to this problem. She does everything she can to make the problems easier to understand. Then she teaches students to do the same thing. She says, "An algebra problem only looks difficult at first. You must relax and read it over several times. Then it will seem less difficult." Another way she says you can make the problem easier is to ask for help.

Sentence	My Paraphrase
Some students find algebra to be something that they could do without.	Some students don't like algebra.

Milestones A • Copyright © Heinle

Name _____ Date _____

● Text Genre

Use with student book page 34.

Informational Text: Internet Article

Web Site	
Web address	the location of the Web site on the Internet; for example: **www.tx.gov**
link	connection to another part of the Web site or another Web address; these words in these links are usually in blue type

A. Review the parts of the Web page below. Focus on the Web address and the links. Then complete the three blank Web pages. Include a Web address and a link. Draw or write in the information section of your web pages. You can use real information from the Internet, or you can make up information.

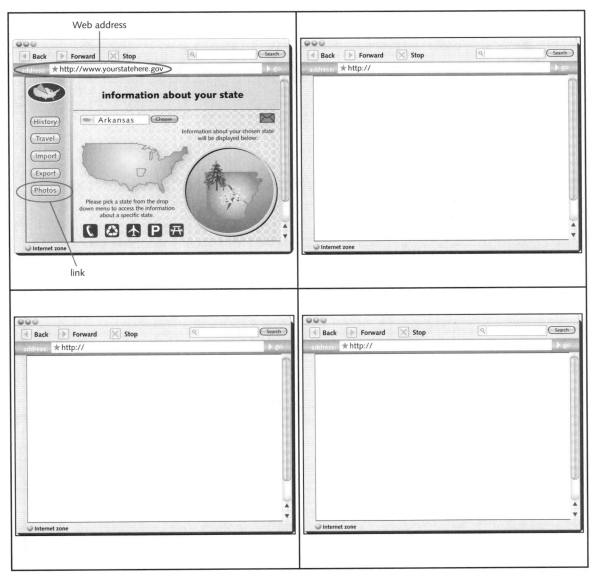

Name _____   Date _____

● Reading Comprehension

Use with student book page 41.

Academic Vocabulary for the Reading Comprehension Questions	
Word	**Explanation**
purpose	a goal, a reason for doing something
inform	to give information about something
entertain	to amuse, to give enjoyment

A. Retell the reading. When you paraphrase, your purpose is to say what you read in your own words so that you will remember the information better. Paraphrase the most important ideas of "Genes: A Family Inheritance."

_____

_____

_____

_____

B. Write your response. How well did "Genes: A Family Inheritance" inform you about how genes work? What facts about your family can you explain by using the information in the reading?

_____

_____

_____

_____

C. Assess the reading strategy. Did your paraphrase help you understand "Genes: A Family Inheritance" better? Why or why not?

_____

_____

_____

_____

Name _____ Date _____

● **Text Elements**

Use with student book page 41.

Visuals and Captions

- A **visual** is a photograph, illustration, chart, or map. It gives more information about a text.
- **Captions** are the words under a visual. They explain the information in the visual.

A. Make a chart listing some of your family members. List two older than you, two the same age as you, and two younger than you.

How Old	Names
older	

B. What is the best caption for this chart?

   a. How Old I Am
   b. Ages of My Family Members
   c. My Favorite Family Members

C. Make a drawing of the youngest person in your family.

D. What is the best caption for this drawing?

   a. Young and Old
   b. The Origin of My Family
   c. The Newest Family Member

Name _____ Date _____

● Vocabulary From the Reading

Use with student book page 42.

> **Key Vocabulary**
>
> hero   serious
> honest   truth
> proud

A. Complete each sentences. Use one of the Key Vocabulary words in each sentence.

Example: Does she ever stop laughing?

         Yes, she does. Sometimes she is _____*serious*_____.

1. What do you call a man who always tells the truth?

   He is an _____ man.

2. Do you ever lie?

   No, I always tell the _____.

3. What is the opposite of **silly**?

   The opposite of **silly** is _____.

4. Jack saved the baby's life.

   Jack is a _____ to the baby's family.

5. How did Jack feel after he saved the baby's life?

   He felt _____.

B. Answer the questions. Use as many of the Key Vocabulary words as you can.

1. Name a person who is a hero to you.

   _____

2. Why is this person a hero?

   _____

3. Is it OK to feel good about yourself when you do something good?

   _____

Name _____ Date _____

● Reading Strategy
Draw Conclusions

Use with student book page 43.

> Sometimes writers give you clues or hints that help you **draw conclusions** about the characters and events in a story.

A. Read the passage and answer the questions.

Ken is standing outside the classroom door. He is holding his car keys in his hand. In the room, Nina is talking with the teacher. She can't see Ken. Ken is smiling at her. She starts to turn to go, and he steps back from the door. When she comes out into the hall, Ken says, "Oh, hi Nina. I didn't know you were still here."

1. What reasons might Ken have for standing by the classroom door? Try to think of three possible reasons.

   _____

   _____

   _____

2. Which reason do you think is true?

   _____

3. What clues in the passage lead you to this conclusion?

   _____

   _____

B. Read each situation. Then read the three sentences. Which sentence is the best conclusion that you can draw from the situation?

1. You come home and your family is watching television. Everyone is laughing.

   a. They are telling jokes.

   b. They are happy because it is Saturday.

   c. They are watching a comedy show.

2. You have a math test today. You studied chapter 5 last night. When you look at the test, you see that it is on chapter 6. Which sentence is the best conclusion that you can draw from the situation?

   a. Your teacher will let you take the test tomorrow.

   b. You won't make a very good grade.

   c. You should study harder.

Name _____ Date _____

● **Text Genre**

Use with student book page 43.

Biography

Biography	
events	important things that happened in the person's life
other people	people who were important in the person's life
descriptions	details about the times and places in the person's life

A. Read the passage. Then label the sentences listed below it. Use the words **events, other people,** and **descriptions.**

Martina Navratilova

(1) Tennis star Martina Navratilova was born in Prague, the capital of the Czech Republic, in 1956. (2) She later moved to a small town in the countryside called Revnice. (3) Navratilova's grandmother, Agnes Semenska, had been a famous tennis player. (4) Navratilova used her grandmother's racket when she first started playing tennis.

(5) Navratilova's stepfather, Miroslav Navratil, was her first teacher. (6) He encouraged her to become a strong and disciplined player. (7) She began playing in tennis tournaments when she was only eight years old. (8) When she was 17, she became the number one player in her country. (9) Two years later, in August 1975, Navratilova applied to become an American citizen.

(10) Life in the United States was not easy for her at first. (11) She missed her parents, she gained a lot of weight, and she lost many games. (12) However, she soon made new friends and started to feel happier and play better. (13) Finally, on July 8, 1978, she won Wimbledon! (14) She became the number one female tennis player in the world.

Example: Sentence 1 ____*descriptions*_____

1. Sentence 3 _____

2. Sentence 5 _____

3. Sentence 8 _____

4. Sentence 9 _____

5. Sentence 11 _____

6. Sentence 13 _____

Name _____ Date _____

● Reading Comprehension

Use with student book page 47.

A. **Retell the story.** Be sure to include these things: an important event in Roberto Clemente's life; a person who was important in his life; some details about a time or place in his life.

_____

_____

_____

_____

_____

_____

_____

B. **Write your response.** What conclusions did you draw about Roberto Clemente as you read? Do you recognize anything about Roberto Clemente's family that is similar to your family? Explain.

_____

_____

_____

_____

_____

C. **Assess the reading strategy.** How does drawing conclusions about a character or event help you understand and remember what you are reading?

_____

_____

_____

_____

_____

Name _____ Date _____

● Spelling
Irregular Noun Plurals

Use with student book page 47.

There are several types of irregular noun plurals, for example, the words **men** and **children** from the readings in this unit. To form the plural of some irregular nouns, such as **man,** you must change the vowel. Other irregular nouns, such as **child,** change their forms completely. A few nouns have the same singular and plural forms.

Vowel Change		Different Forms		No change	
Singular	**Plural**	**Singular**	**Plural**	**Singular**	**Plural**
man	men	child	children	fish	fish
woman	women	person	people	sheep	sheep
foot	feet	octopus	octopi	scissors	scissors
tooth	teeth	mouse	mice	series	series

A. Circle the correct form.

Example: The three (childs /(children)) are watching TV.

1. There are three (womans / women) in the store.

2. Did your (feet / foots) hurt after you walked home?

3. Can I borrow your (scissor / scissors)?

4. Dad says we have (mouses / mice) in our garage.

5. I caught two (fish / fishes) yesterday.

6. How many (sheep / sheeps) were in the field?

B. Write five sentences about things you have done or seen. Use an irregular plural in each sentence.

Example: _I saw three deer in our back yard._____

1. _____

2. _____

3. _____

4. _____

5. _____

Milestones A • Copyright © Heinle

Name _____ Date _____

● Writing Conventions
Use with student book page 47.
Punctuation: Identifying Titles of Documents

There are three ways to show the title of a document: quotation marks, underlining, or italics.

Quotation Marks	Used for the titles of songs, TV shows, short stories, essays, and poems; also used for the title of one part of a larger work, for example, a chapter in a book or an article in a newspaper.
Underlining or Italics	Used for a complete written work such as a whole book, a play, a newspaper, a magazine, or a movie.

A. Use quotation marks or underlining to identify the following titles.

Example: Linda Lewis is making a new movie called <u>Time Out for Fun</u>.

1. Do you watch The News at Nine on TV?

2. I read an essay entitled Why I Sing.

3. Our school put on the play A Teenage Musical last month.

4. Have you seen the movie Star Wars yet?

B. List the names of the items described below. Use correct punctuation for each.

Example: A newspaper you read <u>The Houston Chronicle</u>

1. Your favorite magazine _____

2. A newspaper article you read _____

3. A movie you liked _____

4. Your favorite song _____

5. A book you own _____

C. Circle the places where quotation marks and underlining are needed. Then rewrite the sentences correctly.

   I wrote a poem called The Road. I got the idea from a poem, The Road Not Taken, by Robert Frost. My poem was published in our school newspaper, Student Days.

_____

_____

_____

Name _____ Date _____

● Vocabulary Development

Use with student book page 49.

Word Origins: Greek Roots

Look at these Greek roots and their meanings.

Greek Root	Meaning	Greek Root	Meaning	Greek Root	Meaning
bio	life	meter	measure	cent	hundred
graph	write	cycle	wheel	phone	sound
ology	study of	micro	small	scope	see
		tele	far	thermo	heat

A. Answer these questions. Use one or more Greek roots in each answer. Check a dictionary to determine the exact spellings.

Example: What device helps you <u>see</u> <u>small</u> things?   A *microscope*

1. What is something that <u>measures</u> <u>heat</u>?   A _____

2. What is the <u>study</u> of <u>music</u>?   A _____

3. What is the <u>study</u> of living things?   A _____

4. What device sends <u>sound</u> to <u>far</u> places?   A _____

5. What is the <u>study</u> of hand<u>writing</u>?   A _____

6. What is like a bicycle but has only <u>one</u> <u>wheel</u>?   A _____

    (Hint: *uni = one*)

B. Look up some Greek roots in a dictionary. Find some other words with these roots. Write each word along with its meaning.

Example: _tricycle_   _three wheels_

1. _____   _____

2. _____   _____

3. _____   _____

Name _____ Date _____

● Grammar

Use with student book page 50.

The Simple Present Tense

Simple Present Tense	
subject	verb
I	work.
He / She / It	works.
You / We / They	work.

1. When the subject is **he**, **she**, or **it**, add an **s** to the verb. (work / work**s**)
2. When the verb ends in **ss**, **sh**, **ch**, **x**, or **z**, add **es**. (wash / wash**es**)
3. When the verb ends in consonant + **y**, change **y** to **i** and add **es**. (cry / cr**ies**)

A. Check each sentence that contains a simple present tense verb.

Example: ___✔___ They live in Portland.

1. _____ I walked home yesterday.

2. _____ Susan cleans her room every Saturday.

3. _____ We run really fast.

4. _____ They are doing homework.

5. _____ I wait for the bus at the corner.

B. Complete each sentence. Use the correct form of the verb in parentheses.

Example: Ming _____*draws*_____ beautiful pictures. (draw)

1. We _____ soccer on Saturday. (play)

2. John _____ in the evening. (study)

3. I _____ near the school. (live)

4. The sun _____ every day. (shine)

5. Mother _____ dinner most nights. (cook)

Name _____ Date _____

C. Rewrite the sentences. Use the word in parentheses to replace the original subject.

Example: They come from Mexico. (she) _She comes from Mexico._

1. I live in Texas. (he) _____

2. We wear blue jeans. (they) _____

3. They finish at noon. (it) _____

4. We watch a lot of TV. (she) _____

5. I work after school. (they) _____

6. We try to arrive early. (he) _____

7. You like pizza. (I) _____

8. I know the answer. (she) _____

D. Complete the answers. Use full sentences.

Example: **Q:** What kind of car does your teacher drive?

    A: _My teacher drives a Honda._

1. **Q:** How much does a hamburger cost?
    A: _____

2. **Q:** Where does your best friend live?
    A: _____

3. **Q:** Where does your mother work?
    A: _____

E. What do you do every day? Write full sentences. Use the simple present tense.

1. _____

2. _____

3. _____

4. _____

Name _____ Date _____

● Grammar Expansion

Yes/No Questions in the Simple Present Tense

Use **do** or **does** + the base form of the verb to make questions in the simple present tense.

do or *does*	subject	base verb	
Do	I		
Does	he / she / it	run	fast?
Do	you / we / they		

A. Unscramble the words and phrases to make questions.

Example: like / you / do / video games

    Do you like video games?

1. your teacher / give / a lot of homework / does

   _____

2. do / learn quickly / the students

   _____

3. you and your sister / watch / television at night / do

   _____

4. I / do / a haircut / need

   _____

5. does / work / your telephone

   _____

B. Fill in the blanks with **do** or **does**.

Example: _____ *Do* _____ you hear that funny noise?

1. _____ your older brother have a car?

2. _____ the soccer players need some water?

3. _____ your father work on weekends?

4. _____ Ms. Diaz give difficult tests?

Name _____   Date _____

● Grammar Expansion
Negative Statements in the Simple Present Tense

Use **do not** or **does not** + the base form of the verb to make negative statements in the simple present tense.

subject	*does not* or *do not*	base verb	
I	**do not**		
She / He / It	**does not**	like	loud music.
We / You / They	**do not**		

A. Complete the sentences with **do not** or **does not**.

Example: I _____*do not*_____ eat fried food very often.

1. My brother and I _____ enjoy playing video games.

2. Sara _____ go to the movies very often.

3. Our teachers _____ want us to fail.

4. Our neighborhood _____ have a swimming pool.

5. This ice cream _____ taste very good.

B. Rewrite these positive statements to make them negative.

Example: I take the bus to school. _I do not take the bus to school._

1. Rosa likes fish. _____

2. My computer works well. _____

3. My parents take the bus to work. _____

4. Our team wins every time. _____

C. Write two sentences about things you **do not** like. Write two sentences about things that a friend **does not** like.

1. _____

2. _____

3. _____

4. _____

Name ——————————————————————— Date ———————————————

● Writing Assignment

Use with student book page 52.

Descriptive Writing: Write a Paragraph About Yourself

Fill in this chart to help you prepare for writing your descriptive paragraph.

1. List some adjectives that describe your **appearance.** These words tell how you look.   **Example:** tall
2. Write some sentences with details about your **appearance.**   **Example:** I always wear black running shoes.
3. List some adjectives that describe your **personality.** These words tell how you act.   **Example:** quiet
4. Write some sentences with details about your **personality.**   **Example:** My friends say I'm funny.
5. You should get the reader's attention with the first sentence. Write some possible first sentences.   **Example:** I was in school for three months before I spoke to anyone.

Name _____ Date _____

● Writing Assignment
Writing Support

Use with student book page 53.

> **Grammar: Adjectives**
>
> **Use and Placement**
>
> **Adjectives** are words that describe nouns. Be careful to put adjectives in the right place in a sentence.
>
> Adjectives come before nouns.   I have a **loud** voice.
>
> Adjectives can also come after the verb **be.**   My voice is **loud.**

A. Use the words to write sentences.

Example: red / he / car / a / drives
He drives a red car.
_____

1. like / ice cream / chocolate / we

   _____

2. my / is / tall / mother

   _____

3. wants / bicycle / Anna / a / red

   _____

4. new / need / shoes / I

   _____

5. beautiful / flowers / the / are

   _____

B. Tell about people you know. Use sentences with adjectives.

Example: _My sister is tall. She likes sad movies._

1. _____

2. _____

3. _____

4. _____

Name _____ Date _____

● Writing Assignment
Revising Activity

Use with student book page 53.

Read each revision tip. Then rewrite the sentences to make them better.

Revision Tip # 1: Be sure to start your paragraph with an interesting sentence.

First Try	A Better Way to Say It
Example: I was born on February 11, 1993.	I was born in the middle of a snowstorm on February 11, 1993.
1. My family comes from Mexico.	
2. I like basketball.	

Revision Tip # 2: Use information about your appearance and personality.

First Try	A Better Way to Say It
1. I like nice clothes.	
2. I'm short.	
3. I'm friendly.	

Revision Tip # 3: Use details and descriptive words.

First Try	A Better Way to Say It
1. I'm a good soccer player.	
2. I get good grades.	
3. My best friend is nice.	

Name _____   Date _____

● Writing Assignment
Editing Activity

Use with student book page 53.

Read the paragraph. The letters show where there are problems.

(1) I was born in June. The date was June 25, 1992. I have two older brothers. (2) The town I lived in was pretty unusual. (3) We lived there for a few years. (4) My father worked in a factory big. He left the house at 7:00 in the morning and came home after I was in bed. That wasn't great. But he always played soccer with me on Saturday mornings. (5) He still talk about how much fun it was.

A.   Match each letter with the name of the problem.

Example: __e__ Sentence #1

a. There is a problem with the adjective.

1. _____ Sentence #2

b. There is a problem with the verb.

2. _____ Sentence #3

c. It needs details of time.

3. _____ Sentence #4

d. It needs details of place.

4. _____ Sentence #5

e. ~~The writer needs to get the reader's attention~~.

B.   Now fix the problems. Rewrite sentences #1, #4, and #5. Write new sentences for #2 and #3.

1. _____

2. _____

3. _____

4. _____

5. _____

Name _____ Date _____

Vocabulary From the Reading

Use with student book page 70.

> **Key Vocabulary**
>
> burn   melt
> ceremony   relative
> freeze   wonder
> located

A. Match each Key Vocabulary word with the correct definition.

Example: __b__ relative

1. _____ ceremony
2. _____ freeze
3. _____ located
4. _____ melt
5. _____ burn
6. _____ wonder

a. to change from solid to liquid
b. ~~person connected through blood or marriage to someone else~~
c. found in a particular spot or position
d. to think about with curiosity
e. formal event that follows traditions or customs
f. to change from liquid to solid
g. to be on fire; to damage with fire

B. Complete each sentence with one of the Key Vocabulary words.

Example: My favorite __relative__ is Aunt Marie.

1. My school is _____ on Bay Avenue.
2. An ice cube will _____ in a cup of hot water.
3. This candle will _____ for at least two hours.
4. I _____ how old Mrs. Baker is.
5. Did the water in the lake _____ last winter?
6. We took pictures of my sister's wedding _____.

C. Write sentences like those in Exercise B. Write about your own life.

Example: __I like to freeze juice and then eat it.__

1. _____
2. _____
3. _____

Name _____ Date _____

● Reading Strategy

Use with student book page 71.

Make Predictions

When you **make predictions**, you guess what will happen next. As you read, you can **revise** and **confirm** your predictions.

Academic Vocabulary for the Reading Strategy	
Word	Explanation
revise	to change something already written in order to make corrections or to improve it
confirm	to make sure something is right by checking it

A. Read the paragraph.

Three friends are trying to decide what to do tonight. Lisa wants to go out for pizza, and David wants to see a movie. Sammy wants them to go to his house and listen to music. He can't go out because he doesn't have any money.

What do you think the three friends will do? Why?

_____

B. Read the paragraph.

A few minutes later, Maria joins the three friends. She wants to go to a great new Mexican restaurant. David and Lisa love the idea. Sammy says he can't come. David offers to pay for Sammy's dinner. He says Sammy can pay him back later.

Now revise the prediction you made in Exercise B.

_____

C. Read the paragraph.

Maria says it's her birthday. Her parents told her they would take her and some friends out for dinner. That is their birthday gift to her.

Now confirm the predictions you made in Exercise A and Exercise B. Revise your prediction again.

_____

Name _____ Date _____

Use with student book page 72.

● **Text Genre**
Play

Play	
scene	a part of a play that happens in one place and at one time
act	a group of two or more scenes that make up a major part of the play; short plays sometimes only have scenes and no acts
narrator	the character who describes the scene and gives background information
stage directions	notes within the play that tell characters how to speak and move

Read these excerpts from a play.

Act One

Narrator: The year is 1952. We see a farmhouse living room. Grandpa is reading the newspaper as his grandson enters the room.

Scene 1: Early morning.

Peter: (*Enters from stage left.*) Hi. What's happening? I just…

_____

Scene 2: Several years later.

Narrator: Several years have passed. Peter has…

Write **T** for **true** and **F** for **false**.

Example: __F__ The narrator's name is Peter.

_____ 1.   Act One has two scenes.

_____ 2.   Scene Two takes place on the same day as Scene One.

_____ 3.   The narrator says, "Early morning."

_____ 4.   "Enters from stage left" is an example of stage directions.

Name _____ Date _____

● Reading Comprehension

Use with student book page 79.

Academic Vocabulary for the Reading Comprehension Questions	
Word	Explanation
perspective	a way of seeing things
reflect	to think deeply about

A. **Retell the play.** Retell *The Strongest One* in your own words. Include the main points of the plot.

_____

_____

_____

_____

_____

_____

_____

B. **Write your response.** Describe the play from the Little Red Ant's perspective. How do you think he felt before, during, and after his travels?

_____

_____

_____

_____

C. **Assess the reading strategy.** How does making predictions help you understand a text better?

_____

_____

_____

_____

Name _____ Date _____

● Literary Element

Use with student book page 79.

Dialogue

> **Dialogue** is the words that characters in a play say to each other.
> The words follow each character's name.

A. Rewrite the sentences in the dialogue form used in plays.

Example: Paul asked, "How old is Susan?"
      Paul: How old is Susan?

1. Ms. Kirk says, "I want to buy a new car."

_____

2. Carlos said, "You should study harder."

_____

3. Ben shouted, "Don't call me Benny!"

_____

4. Linda asked, "Can you lend me some money?"

_____

5. Mr. Carter said, "Please don't leave home."

_____

B. Correct these lines of dialogue. Use the editing marks on page 419 of your student book.

1. Pete: can I borrow your pen?
2. Mother: "Don't forget your backpack!"
3. Policeman, this little boy is lost.
4. Doctor this will make you feel better

C. Write two lines of dialogue of your own. You can use friends' or family members' names if you wish.

1. _____

2. _____

Name _____ Date _____

● Vocabulary From the Reading

Use with student book page 80.

Key Vocabulary

circular   distance
consist   ratio

A. Write the Key Vocabulary word for each definition.

Word	Definition
Example: _consist_	to be made up of something or some things
1. _____	the space between two things
2. _____	how one thing compares to another thing
3. _____	having a round shape

B. Complete the sentences. Use a different Key Vocabulary word in each sentence.

Example: It's a long ____distance____ from here to Los Angeles.

1. The _____ of boys to girls in this class is two to one.

2. Does the class _____ of mostly boys?

3. The clock on the wall isn't square. It's _____ .

4. What is the _____ from the earth to the moon?

C. Rewrite the sentences. Use Key Vocabulary words in place of the **boldfaced** words.

Example: What is the **relationship** between male soldiers and female soldiers?
    What is the ratio of male soldiers to female soldiers?

1. The **length** between these houses is very small.

    _____

2. The house had unusual **round** windows.

    _____

3. The **measurement** between the trees was ten feet.

    _____

Name _____ Date _____

● Reading Strategy
Talk Through a Problem

Use with student book page 81.

> When you do math, **talk through the problem.**
> 1. Describe the problem in your own words to a partner.
> 2. Decide how to solve the problem.
> 3. Try to solve the problem out loud.

Here is a math problem:

There are 30 students in the class. You are ordering pizza for a party. Everyone should get at least two pieces of pizza. Each pie is divided into eight pieces. How many pizzas should you order?

A. Describe the problem in your own words.

_____

_____

B. Tell how you would solve the problem.

_____

_____

C. List the steps to solve the problem.

1. _____

2. _____

3. _____

4. _____

5. _____

6. _____

Name _____ Date _____

● Text Genre
Textbook

Use with student book page 81.

Math Textbook Features	
chapter headings	names of chapters; they tell you what the chapter is about; they also help you find information in the book
words in bold	heavy, dark type for important words; sometimes these words are also in color
examples	problems with answers given to help students understand how to solve the problem
exercises	problems for students to solve by themselves

A. Read this example from a math textbook.

> **Explanation:**
> The radius of a circle is half of the diameter. To find the radius, you divide the diameter by the number two.

B. Circle words in the explanation above that should be in **bold** type.

C. Here is another example from a math textbook. Circle the words that should be in **bold** type.

> **Explanation:**
> To find an average, you add and then divide. To find the average of five numbers, you add up all the numbers and divide by five.

D. Write an explanation of something you know. Circle the words that should be in **bold** type.

_____

_____

_____

_____

_____

_____

_____   _____

● Reading Comprehension   *Use with student book page 85.*

A. Tell what you learned. Which math skills did you learn about in the reading?

_____

_____

_____

_____

_____

_____

B. Write your response. Were the step-by-step instructions helpful? Were you able to follow those instructions?

_____

_____

_____

_____

_____

C. Assess the reading strategy. How does talking through a math problem help you solve it?

_____

_____

_____

_____

Name _____ Date _____

● Spelling

Use with student book page 85.

Apostrophes with Possessive Nouns

Add an **apostrophe + s** to a singular noun and most irregular plural nouns to show ownership.

> Is this **Pedro's** bike?
> These are my **sister's** sons.
> Those are the **children's** toys

After a regular plural noun ending in **s**, you add only an **apostrophe** to show ownership.

> This is my **parents'** car.
> Those are my **friends'** bicycles.

A. Complete each sentence with the possessive form of the noun in parentheses.

Example: Is that _____*Paul's*_____ dictionary? (Paul)

1. Have you seen _____ purse? (Sally)

2. Where are the _____ uniforms? (girls)

3. Did you see that _____ eyes? (woman)

4. She keeps a list of the _____ addresses. (employees)

5. Don't go too close to the _____ edge. (water)

6. Many of my _____ houses are white. (neighbors)

B. Use the two words below to write sentences with possessive nouns.

Example: (winter / wind) __*Winter's winds are cold.*__

1. (the singer / voice) _____

2. (my friends / parents) _____

3. (John / vacation) _____

4. (the dogs / collars) _____

5. (Colorado / mountains) _____

6. (her sister / toy) _____

Name _____ Date _____

● Writing Conventions

Use with student book page 85.

Punctuation: Colons in Plays, Speeches, and Interviews

In interviews and speeches, a colon goes after the speakers' names. Quotation marks are not used.

Interviewer:	And how many countries did you visit, Mr. Lee?
Mr. Lee:	Thirty-seven or thirty-eight, I believe.
Dr. Hill:	It's a pleasure to present Senator Baker.
Senator Baker:	Thank you for inviting me today, Dr. Hill.

In plays, the scene number and the names of the characters who are speaking are followed by a colon.

Scene 3: The Ants' Hole

Narrator: So Little Red Ant went back home and spoke to the ant people.
Second Ant: Little Red Ant has returned.
Third Ant: He has come back alive!

A. Use colons as you rewrite the following text.

Bill is interviewing the school principal, Mrs. Landry. He asks, "What advice do you have for students?" She answers, "It's really important to make the most of your vacation time."

_____

_____

_____

B. Use colons as you rewrite the following text.

The first scene of a play is a cage in a zoo. The narrator says, "The monkeys are talking quietly among themselves." The first monkey says, "I think we should wait until it's really dark."

_____

_____

_____

Name _____ Date _____

● Vocabulary Development

Use with student book page 87.

Word Origins: Latin Root Words

Latin Root Word	Meaning	English Words from This Chapter
circ	round, around	**circ**le, **circ**umference, **circ**ular
dict	speak	pre**dict**ion
form	form, shape	**form**ula
frac	break	**frac**tion
loc	place	**loc**ated

A. Use a word from the chart to complete each sentence.

Example: The teacher will _____*dictate*_____ the words and we will write
them.

1. The shape of the park has no corners. It's _____.

2. Can he really make a _____ about what will happen
twenty-five years from now?

3. I got most of the test questions right. I only got a _____ of
them wrong.

4. The _____ of my house is behind that store.

5. The distance around a circle is its _____.

6. This is the right _____ to solve that math problem.

B. Choose five words from the chart and write a sentence using each one.

1. _____

2. _____

3. _____

4. _____

5. _____

Milestones A • Copyright © Heinle

Name _____ Date _____

● Grammar

Use with student book page 88.

Subject and Object Pronouns

Subject Pronouns	
I	I know him.
you	You need her.
he	He asks you.
she	She visits us.
it	It likes her.
we	We see them.
they	They help you.

Object Pronouns	
me	He knows me.
you	She needs you.
him	You ask him.
her	We visit her.
it	She likes it.
us	They see us.
them	You help them.

A. Rewrite these sentences using subject pronouns.

Example: The ants live in the desert. __They live in the desert.__

1. *The Strongest One* is an interesting play.

   _____

2. The characters are ants.

   _____

3. Anna likes the play.

   _____

4. Gabriella and I are interested in ants.

   _____

B. Complete each sentence. Use the correct object pronoun for the underlined word or words.

Example: My <u>sister</u> is in class. I am waiting for _____*her*_____.

1. This <u>sandwich</u> is great! I like _____.

2. My <u>parents</u> have a store. I help _____ in the store.

3. <u>You</u> need help. I will help _____.

4. <u>Pete and I</u> talked in class. The teacher saw _____.

Name _____ Date _____

● Grammar Expansion
Compound Subjects and Objects

Sentences can have two or more subjects and objects. These are called **compound subjects** and **compound objects**.

Compound Subjects	Compound Objects
My brother and I do our homework	with **Miguel** and **Rosa**.

1. When using compound subjects and compound objects with pronouns, be sure to use the correct pronoun.

   Correct: Yuri and **I** went to the movies.
   Incorrect: Yuri and **me** went to the movies.

   Correct: Joe went to the movies with Alex and **me**.
   Incorrect: Joe went to the movies with Alex and **I**.

2. If **I** is in a compound subject pronoun, put it last.

   Correct: Jenny and I like spaghetti.
   Incorrect: I and Jenny like spaghetti.

A. Underline the pronoun errors in these sentences. Then write the sentences correctly.

Example: My friend and <u>me</u> always play basketball on Saturdays.

My friend and I always play basketball on Saturdays.

1. The teacher had a talk with Ricardo and I.

_____

2. Him and Denise did their homework together.

_____

3. Me and my father like to go bowling together.

_____

4. Do you know Nancy? I saw she and Ali at the mall.

_____

5. Him and me always ride our bikes home after school.

_____

Name _____ Date _____

● Grammar
Imperatives

Use with student book page 89.

Imperatives					
affirmative			negative		
base form of verb			*don't*	base form of verb	
Open	the door.		Don't	open	the door.

A. Match each statement with an affirmative or negative imperative to give advice or a warning.

Statements

Example: __c__ I have a sore throat.

1. _____ I am very tired.

2. _____ This is a very big sandwich.

3. _____ This shirt is very expensive.

4. _____ I have a big test tomorrow.

5. _____ I don't know where my wallet is.

6. _____ This knife is very sharp.

Imperatives

a. Study a lot tonight.

b. Don't eat too much.

c. Drink some tea with honey.

d. Don't buy it.

e. Look under the sofa.

f. Don't cut yourself.

g. Take a nap.

B. You are taking care of some small children on a playground. Imagine what they are doing. Write two affirmative imperatives and two negative imperatives that you would say to them.

Examples: Hit the ball!

Don't fall down!

1. _____

2. _____

3. _____

4. _____

Name _____ Date _____

● Grammar Expansion

Polite Imperatives

When you use an imperative to make a request, use the polite form.

Polite Imperatives				
Positive	Please		open	the door.
Negative	Please	don't	open	the door.

Please can go at the beginning or the end of the sentence. If **please** is at the end, put a comma before it.

> **Please** open the door.
> Open the door, **please**.

A. Read each sentence. Then write a polite request you might make for each situation.

Example: You want Bill to call you this evening.

Please call me this evening.

1. You want someone to help wash the dishes.

_____

2. You want someone to listen to you.

_____

3. You want someone to wait for you.

_____

4. You want someone to come back later.

_____

5. You don't want someone to call you after 10:00 in the evening.

_____

B. You are giving a birthday party for a friend. Write four polite commands that you might say to your guests.

Example: _____ *Please come in.* _____

1. _____

2. _____

3. _____

4. _____

Milestones A • Copyright © Heinle

Name _____ Date _____

● Writing Assignment
Creative Writing: Write a Scene

Use with student book pages 90–91.

A. Brainstorm a list of new characters you might add to the scene.

New Character	Brief Description
River	_River is afraid of the dam._

B. Choose three of your characters for Little Red Ant to speak with. Explain why each one might think the next one is stronger.

New Character	Why This Character Might Think the Next One Is Stronger

Name _____ Date _____

● Writing Assignment
Writing Support

Use with student book page 91.

Mechanics: Capitalization

1. Use a capital letter for the first letter of the first word of a sentence.
   Good writers capitalize words correctly.

2. Use a capital letter for the pronoun **I**.
   My mother and **I** went shopping yesterday.

3. Use capital letters for proper nouns including the names of people, holidays, days of the week, and months.
   John celebrates **T**hanksgiving on the third **T**hursday of every **N**ovember.

4. Use capital letters for the first word and all important words in the titles of books, plays, movies, TV shows, works of art, musical compositions, and organizations.
   The Strongest One   "The Star-Spangled Banner"

A. Rewrite these sentences. Use capital letters where necessary.

Example: my favorite months are july and august.

My favorite months are July and August. _____

1. anna and i bought birthday presents for my father.

   _____

2. memorial day comes in may and labor day comes in september.

   _____

3. i love the movie *star wars*.

   _____

4. on monday, we visited the san diego zoo.

   _____

5. we went to see the *mona lisa* at the louvre museum in paris.

   _____

B. Write about a television show. Tell the name of the show, what day it is on, and the names of the characters and the actors. Tell if you liked the show or not. Make sure to use correct capitalization in your writing.

   _____

   _____

   _____

   _____

Name _____ Date _____

● Writing Assignment
Revising Activity

Use with student book page 91.

Look at this first draft of a scene. It contains some errors in the dialog.

Mr. Grasshopper: I have very strong legs. (**Example:**) <u>Looking at me.</u> See how I can jump. I'm sure I am the strongest of all.

(1) **house fly**: *[Talking to Mouse.]* I think Mr. Grasshopper is the strongest, too. (2) <u>Mr. Grasshopper can jump ten feet in the air.</u>

Mr. Grasshopper: You're right. (3) <u>Please to tell Little Red Ant that I am the strongest.</u>

(4) <u>Then Little Red Ant says, I need to think.</u>

What is the best way to revise each part of the scene?

Example: __b__

    a. Please looking at me.
    b. Look at me.
    c. Look please at me.

Item 1 _____

    a. **House Fly—**
    b. **House fly:**
    c. **House Fly:**

Item 2 _____

    a. He can jump ten feet in the air.
    b. Mr. Grasshopper is jumping ten feet in the air.
    c. Mr. grasshopper can jump ten feet in the air.

Item 3 _____

    a. Please you tell Little Red Ant that I am the strongest.
    b. Please tell Little Red Ant that the strongest is I.
    c. Please tell Little Red Ant that I am the strongest.

Item 4 _____

    a. Little Red Ant says, "I need to think."
    b. Little Red Ant: I need to think.
    c. Then Little Red Ant: "I need to think."

Name _____   Date _____

● Writing Assignment
Editing Activity

Use with student book page 91.

A.   Read this scene and find the mistakes. Mark the mistakes using the editing marks on page 419 of your student book.

Narrator— Bobby lived in a big house with his family. One day he decided to take a walk with his dog, brownie.

Bobby— Hey, Uncle Mac! I'm going to take Brownie for a walk. Please to come with us.

Uncle Mac— Not today, Bobby. Asking Aunt Helen. She likes to take walks.

Bobby— I already asked her. She's going to david's house to help he clean out the garage.

Uncle Mac— She is? Well, maybe I will go with you. To wait a minute while I put on my walking shoes.

Bobby: Sure thing!

B.   Now rewrite the scene. Make the changes you marked above.

_____

_____

_____

_____

_____

_____

_____

_____

_____

Milestones A • Copyright © Heinle

Name _____ Date _____

● Vocabulary From the Reading

Use with student book page 96.

> **Key Vocabulary**
>
> equal   pure
> germ   realize
> mixture   remind

A. Write the Key Vocabulary word for each definition.

Word	Definition
Example: _mixture_	a combination of elements
1. _____	to understand, to start to believe something is true
2. _____	very small living thing that can cause illnesses or disease
3. _____	to be the same as, match
4. _____	to tell someone about something in order to make them remember
5. _____	not mixed with other things

B. Rewrite the sentences using a Key Vocabulary word to replace each word in **bold**.

Example: I didn't **know** you were such a good singer.

I didn't realize you were such a good singer.

1. This **combination** of ingredients is just right.

   _____

2. Do I have to **help you remember** to bring your dictionary every day?

   _____

3. The water in that lake is very **clean**.

   _____

4. One-half and two-fourths are **the same**.

   _____

C. Write your own sentences. Use a Key Vocabulary word in each sentence.

1. _____

2. _____

3. _____

Name _____ Date _____

● Reading Strategy
Use with student book page 97.

Understand Sequence of Events

> The **sequence of events** is the order in which events happen. Understanding the sequence of events can help you **locate** and **focus** on important information.

Academic Vocabulary for the Reading Strategy	
Word	**Explanation**
locate	to find by searching
focus	to center one's attention on

A. Read the paragraph.

   Marta got up at 11:00 on Saturday morning. The sun was shining, and she could see the clear blue sky outside her window. After a few minutes, she went downstairs and looked around. Nobody was home. That seemed strange. She went into the kitchen and poured herself a glass of milk. It was cold and tasted really good. She was still half asleep. As she sat there, the kitchen door slowly opened. Then her whole family ran into the room and shouted, "Happy Birthday!" Marta was so sleepy she had forgotten it was her birthday.

B. Locate the events in the paragraph. List them below.

Example: _Marta got up._

1. _____

2. _____

3. _____

4. _____

C. Focus on the most important event. Why do you think it is more important than the others?

_____

_____

_____

Name _____ Date _____

● **Text Genre**
Informational Text

Use with student book page 98.

Informational Text	
facts	true information about the topic
problems	the author presents a problem
solutions	the author explains how a problem is solved
actual events	things that really happen
dates	when important events happen

Read the passage.

1. Today Europeans buy millions of dollars of products from China each year. But thousands of years ago, there was no easy way for traders to get from Europe to China. The land separating the two countries was very mountainous. Dangerous bands of thieves also threatened anyone who tried to cross this area. The emperor Wu-ti lived from 140 to 87 B.C.E. He helped open a route called the Silk Road. Using this road, some Europeans managed to make the trip and come back with spices, precious gems, and other amazing things.

2. The most famous European to make the trip on this road was Marco Polo. He was from Venice and lived from 1254 to 1324. When he was 17 years old, Marco Polo made his first visit to Beijing, which was called Khanbaligh at that time. He was a very intelligent man and he learned Chinese very quickly. He decided to stay in China, and the emperor made him an important leader.

Complete the chart with facts, problems, solutions, actual events, and dates from the reading above.

Features of the Text	Examples
1. facts	Wu-ti lived from 140 to 87 B.C.E.
2. problems	
3. solutions	
4. actual events	
5. dates	

Name _____ Date _____

● Reading Comprehension

Use with student book page 105.

Academic Vocabulary for the Reading Comprehension Questions	
Word	**Explanation**
evaluate	to study and make a judgment about
speculate	to think about and make a guess

A. **Retell the story.** Choose one of the parts of the reading, "Eureka!" or "Antibiotics." Then choose three important events and write them in the correct sequence in the boxes below.

1. → 2. → 3.

B. **Write your response.** In "Eureka!" the author wrote about three scientists. Which one did you enjoy reading about the most—Archimedes, Newton, or Fleming? Speculate about how this scientist's work changed the world.

_____

_____

_____

_____

_____

C. **Assess the reading strategy.** How does understanding the sequence of events help you understand the reading?

_____

_____

_____

_____

_____

Milestones A • Copyright © Heinle

Name _____ Date _____

● Text Elements

Use with student book page 105.

Writing Style and Tone

- **Writing style** is the author's way of using language. This includes word choice, grammar, sentence length, and punctuation.
- **Tone** is the author's attitude toward the subject and audience. Authors create tone through their writing styles.

A. Read each sentence. Then identify the writing style in each sentence and the tone of the sentence.

Example: The poor little kitten slowly dragged itself up the sidewalk.

_____b_____ Writing Style   _____a_____ Tone
    a. grammar   a. sad
    b. word choice   b. informal
    c. sentence length   c. angry

Sentence #1: Sit down in this chair right here!

1. _____ Writing Style   2. _____ Tone
    a. word choice   a. angry
    b. sentence length   b. formal
    c. punctuation   c. enthusiastic

Sentence #2: The destruction through thermonuclear incidents was devastating.

3. _____ Writing Style   4. _____ Tone
    a. sentence length   a. calm
    b. word choice   b. funny
    c. punctuation   c. serious

Sentence #3: So who cares about history?

5. _____ Writing Style   6. _____ Tone
    a. word choice   a. formal
    b. punctuation   b. thoughtful
    c. sentence length   c. amusing

Sentence #4: We will have to put off the party for . . . a week or two.

7. _____ Writing Style   8. _____ Tone
    a. grammar   a. thoughtful
    b. word choice   b. formal
    c. punctuation   c. excited

Name _____ Date _____

● Vocabulary From the Reading

Use with student book page 106.

> **Key Vocabulary**
> amazed   bud
> bottom   gradually

A. Write the Key Vocabulary word for each definition.

Word	Definition
Example: ___*bottom*___	the lower part, the opposite of the top
1. _____	extremely surprised
2. _____	flower before it opens
3. _____	little by little

B. Answer each question. Use one of the Key Vocabulary words in your answer.

Example: **Q:** Were you surprised to see me at the museum?

   A: Yes, I was ____*amazed*____.

1. **Q:** Are you moving all your furniture to the new apartment at the same time?

   A: No, we're moving it _____.

2. **Q:** What is that little red thing?

   A: It's a rose _____.

3. **Q:** How far down did you swim?

   A: I swam all the way to the _____.

4. **Q:** What did you think of the Empire State Building?

   A: I was _____ at how tall it was.

C. Write sentences about situations in your own life. Use a Key Vocabulary word in each one.

1. _____

2. _____

3. _____

4. _____

Milestones A • Copyright © Heinle

Name _____ Date _____

● Reading Strategy
Recognize Mood in Poetry

Use with student book page 107.

> **Mood** is the feeling the writer wants the reader to get from a reading.

A. Identify the mood of each poem below. Use the words in the box.

amused	~~bored~~	excited	homesick	angry

Example: ____ *bored* ____ The raindrops slipping down my window
Never seem to reach the bottom.
Nothing to do but wait.

1. _____ Why oh why
Did I eat the whole pie?
It tasted good going down
But I think I might die.

2. _____ Walking down the street
Thinking of friends from the past.
Lots of people pass by
Walking really fast.

3. _____ My brother drives by
And doesn't even wave.
What is his problem!
What's wrong with Dave?

4. _____ The soccer team won its match.
The basketball team won its game.
The players are all thrilled
And I'm feeling the same.

B. Choose one of the moods from the box in exercise A, or choose another mood. Write a short poem that expresses this mood.

_____

_____

_____

_____

Name _____ Date _____

● Text Genre

Poetry

Use with student book page 107.

Poetry	
stanzas	groups of lines
images	words and phrases that help readers create pictures in their minds
figurative language	writing that expresses ideas in imaginative ways, such as comparing two things that are not alike

A. A paragraph is a group of sentences in a story or text. What is a group of lines in a poem?

_____

B. Copy the words and phrases below in the correct column of the chart.

- a white, icy day
- coal-black eyes
- gliding like a bird in the sky
- a thought as heavy as a brick
- a mind beginning to blossom
- sleeping like a kitten

Images	Figurative Language
1. a white, icy day	4. _____
2. _____	5. _____
3. _____	6. _____

C. Now make up some images and examples of figurative language of your own.

Images	Figurative Language
1. _____	4. _____
2. _____	5. _____
3. _____	6. _____

Milestones A • Copyright © Heinle

Name _____ Date _____

● **Reading Comprehension**   *Use with student book page 111.*

A. **Get meaning from poetry.** What are the poems "The First Book" and
"Unfolding Bud" about?

_____

_____

_____

_____

_____

_____

_____

B. **Write your response.** What mood did the poems "The First Book" and
"Unfolding Bud" make you feel? Speculate about why the poets chose to
write these poems.

_____

_____

_____

_____

C. **Assess the reading strategy.** Why is it important to recognize the mood of a
poem you are reading?

_____

_____

_____

_____

Name _____   Date _____

● Spelling

Use with student book page 111.

i Before e Except After c

A Spelling Rule	
The basic rule	Write **i** before **e** Except after **c** Or when it sounds like an **a** As in **neighbor** and **weigh**.
Examples of **i** before **e**	believe, chief, field
Examples of **e** before **i** after **c**	deceive, ceiling, receive
Examples of **ei** words pronounced like **a**	eight, freight, neighbor, weigh
Exceptions to the basic rule	either, foreign, height, neither, science

A. Complete each sentence with a word from the chart.

Example: The cows were in a large _____field_____.

1. The _____ was painted white.

2. Biology is my favorite _____ course.

3. I have visited several _____ countries.

4. Did you _____ any e-mails today?

5. Do you _____ in magic?

B. Circle the correct spelling.

Example: What is the ((height) / hieght) of that mountain?

1. My (neighbor / nieghbor) has two dogs.

2. My uncle is a fire (cheif / chief).

3. She is (either / iether) seven or eight years old.

4. How much does you suitcase (weigh / wiegh)?

5. Did the salesperson try to (deceive / decieve) you about the product?

6. I made (ieght / eight) points in the basketball game!

7. There's a dog on the soccer (field / feild).

Name _____ Date _____

● Writing Conventions

Use with student book page 111.

Punctuation: Quotation Marks with Dialogue; Interjections

Quotation Marks with Dialogue	
Rule	**Example**
Place quotation marks before and after the exact words a person says.	Leo said, "He's a great runner."
Punctuation marks usually go inside the quotation marks.	"Where have you been?" she asked. "Let's go now!" he said.

A. Rewrite the information using quotation marks.

Example: Mike asked me where I live. _Mike asked, "Where do you live?"_

1. Paula said she was tired. _____

2. The teacher told us to sit down. _____

3. Chan asked where the library is. _____

4. Ali said he likes cheese. _____

5. My mother asked where my backpack is. _____

Interjections

An **interjection** is a part of speech that shows emotion or surprise.
An **interjection** is usually followed by an exclamation point.

    Wait! I forgot my money.

B. Rewrite the sentences using an exclamation point after each interjection.

Example: Stop. Don't go any further. _Stop! Don't go any further._

1. Run. We're going to be late. _____

2. I think this is the right door. No, wait. _____

3. Calm down. We'll find your wallet. _____

4. Is that new computer yours? You're kidding. _____

Name _____ Date _____

● Vocabulary Development

Use with student book page 113.

Understand Synonyms and Use a Thesaurus

Synonyms are words that have similar meanings. A **thesaurus** is a reference book or online resource that lists synonyms for words.

A. Choose the best synonym for the underlined word.

Example: | **discover** | find out | learn | ~~notice~~ | determine |

When did you <u>discover</u> your glasses were missing? _____*notice*_____

1. | **problem** | difficulty | puzzle | question | trouble |

What's the answer to the second math <u>problem</u>? _____

2. | **flow** | flood | gush | run |

What makes the water <u>flow</u> so slowly? _____

3. | **space** | area | freedom | seat | universe |

Give me some <u>space</u>! _____

4. | **body** | dead person | group | main part | organization |

The <u>body</u> of his essay was well written. _____

5. | **light** | bright | graceful | soft | weightless |

The sun made the room very <u>light</u>. _____

6. | **thing** | device | idea | item | object |

Gravity is the most important <u>thing</u> he discovered. _____

7. | **solution** | answer | explanation | mixture |

He drank a <u>solution</u> of salt and water. _____

8. | **explain** | defend | describe | justify |

Can you <u>explain</u> how the machine works? _____

Name _____ Date _____

● Grammar

Use with student book page 114.

Simple Past Tense of *be*

The Simple Past Tense of *be*		
subject	***be***	
I	**was**	born in 1983.
You	**were**	at home last night.
He / She / It	**was**	cold yesterday.
You / We / They	**were**	in Texas last week.

A. Circle the correct answer.

Example: Archimedes ((was) / were) a genius.

1. The king thought there (was / were) some silver in the crown.

2. Archimedes and Newton (was / were) both scientists.

3. I (was / were) interested in Newton's story.

4. Fleming (was / were) messy in his laboratory.

5. Florey and Chain (was / were) not the discoverers of penicillin.

6. Fleming, Florey, and Chain (was / were) the winners of the Nobel prize in Medicine in 1945.

7. Infections (was / were) very dangerous 100 years ago.

8. Penicillin (was / were) a very important drug.

B. Complete these sentences. Use the simple past tense of **be.** Write true sentences.

Example: Yesterday the weather ___was warm_____.

1. Last night I _____.

2. Last week my friends _____.

3. The teacher _____.

4. The last test _____.

Milestones A • Copyright © Heinle

Name _____ Date _____

● Grammar Expansion
Simple Past of *be:* Negative

To form the negative of the simple past tense of **be,** add **not** after **was** or **were.**

The Simple Past Tense of *be:* Negative		
Subject	***be + not***	
I	was not	born in 1960.
You	were not	at home last Sunday night.
He / She / It	was not	cold last weekend.
We / They	were not	at team practice yesterday.

A. Use the words in parentheses to write negative sentences.

Example: (poet / not / Fleming / was / a)

    <u>Fleming was not a poet.</u>

1. (not / Florey / Chain / were / and / doctors)

    _____

2. (infections / bacterial / not / were / easy to cure)

    _____

3. (factory / lab / Fleming's / not / was / a)

    _____

4. (not / was / poet / a / Archimedes)

    _____

B. Rewrite the sentences. Use the negative form of **be.**

Example: This was my backpack.

    <u>This was not my backpack.</u>

1. The movie was interesting.

    _____

2. My parents were at home last night.

    _____

3. You and I were the last people to leave.

    _____

● Grammar

Use with student book page 115.

The Simple Past Tense

The Simple Past Tense: Affirmative Statements		
subject	**base form of verb + -d / -ed**	
I You He / She / It We They	work**ed** danc**ed** wait**ed**	last night.

A. Circle the simple past tense verbs in these sentences.

Example: We (decided) to go to the movies.

1. It rained yesterday, but now the sun is shining.

2. I like to pick the flowers that we planted.

3. I showed my friends that I know how to cook.

4. We arrived just as they opened the door.

5. They traveled to Asia to visit relatives.

6. I worked very hard on this project.

B. Complete the paragraph with the simple past tense forms of the verbs in parentheses.

Yesterday I _____visited_____ (**Example:** visit) the public library. I

_____ (1. want) to get a library card. I _____ (2. talk) to a

librarian. He was very helpful. He _____ (3. show) me what to do. First

I _____ (4. fill) out an application. Then, I _____ (5. check)

the application carefully to make sure that the information was correct. Finally,

I _____ (6. sign) and _____ (7. date) the application and

_____ (8. hand) it to the librarian. Now I have my library card, and I

check out books every week!

Name _____ Date _____

The Simple Past Tense: Negative Statements			
subject	*did + not*	base form of verb	
I You He / She / It We They	**did not**	work dance wait	last night.

C. Rewrite the sentences. Make simple past tense negative statements.

Example: I worked on Sunday.

_I did not work on Sunday._____

1. Newton explained gravity in the 1500s.

_____

2. Archimedes lived in Italy.

_____

3. Newton discovered penicillin.

_____

4. Fleming turned penicillin into a drug.

_____

5. Bacteria grew on the penicillin.

_____

D. Complete the sentences with the simple past tense affirmative or negative verbs. Tell the truth. Use the verbs in parentheses.

Example: I ____ _did not work_ ____ on my science project last night. (work)

1. I _____ in California last year. (live)

2. My friends _____ me last weekend. (visit)

3. My parents _____ home Saturday night. (stay)

4. It _____ yesterday. (rain)

5. I _____ television last night. (watch)

Milestones A • Copyright © Heinle

Name _____ Date _____

● **Writing Assignment**   *Use with student book pages 116–117.*
Creative Writing: Write a Historical Fiction Paragraph

Use this page to help you prewrite your historical fiction paragraph.

A. Choose a "eureka" moment to write about. Describe this important moment **of** discovery in one sentence.

_____

_____

_____

_____

B. Use the Internet, an encyclopedia, or library books to gather information on the topic. Make notes in the space below.

_____

_____

_____

_____

_____

_____

_____

_____

_____

_____

_____

● **Writing Assignment**   *Use with student book page 117.*
Writing Support

> **Mechanics: Punctuation Marks at the End of Sentences**
>
> **Period (.):**   Use a period at the end of a statement.
>   **Howard Carter discovered King Tutankhamen's tomb.**
> **Question mark (?):**   Use a question mark at the end of a question.
>   **When did he discover the tomb?**
> **Exclamation Point (!):** Use an exclamation point at the end of a sentence to
>   show strong feeling.
>   **At last, I found the tomb!**

A.   Write the correct punctuation mark at the end of each sentence.

Example: Did Benjamin Franklin really discover electricity__?__

1. Stop teasing your little brother right now _____

2. Where were you last Saturday night _____

3. Please take out your notebooks _____

4. I have one brother and one sister _____

5. Is it going to rain _____

6. Don't walk into a busy street _____

7. Do you like action movies _____.

8. Wait _____ I'll go with you.

B.   Fill in sentences that work with the punctuation marks below.

Example: __Do you like big dogs_____?

1. _____.

2. _____!

3. _____.

4. _____!

5. _____?

Name _____ Date _____

● Writing Assignment
Revising Activity

Use with student book page 117.

Study the revision tips below. Then rewrite each example to make it better.

Revision Tip # 1: Add details to make the writing clearer or more interesting.

First Try	A Better Way to Say It
Example: The queen looked at Columbus.	The queen wrinkled her forehead and stared at Columbus.
1. The palace was big.	
2. Columbus was nervous.	
3. Columbus left the room.	

Revision Tip # 2: Rewrite information that is repetitive. Remove information that is unnecessary.

First Try	A Better Way to Say It
4. Columbus was born in a city in Italy. The name of the city was Genoa.	
5. Marco Polo wrote about his trips, and Columbus read about Marco Polo's trips.	
6. Columbus worked for his uncle. His uncle had sailing ships. Columbus enjoyed sailing on his uncle's ships.	

Name _____ Date _____

● Writing Assignment
Editing Activity

Use with student book page 117.

Read this historical fiction paragraph. Mark the mistakes using the editing marks on page 419 of your student book. Then rewrite the scene correctly.

The Discovery of Gravity

One day a scientist named Isaac Newton was sitting under an apple tree. an apple fell and hit him on the head. He been very surprised. He start to wonder what made the apple fall. Why did it fall straight down? why didn't it fall up or sideways. Then he realize something. A force that attracted things down toward the earth. He call this force gravity.

_____

_____

_____

_____

_____

_____

_____

_____

_____

_____

_____

_____

_____

_____

Name _____ Date _____

● Vocabulary From the Reading

Use with student book page 134.

> **Key Vocabulary**
>
> design   rhythm
> disappear   serious
> machine   steep
> merchant

A. Match the underlined Key Vocabulary word with the correct definition.

Example: __e__ Don't you love that rhythm?

1. _____ The bank uses a machine to count money.
2. _____ The sun disappeared around noon.
3. _____ I designed a garden in front of my house.
4. _____ The stairs are very steep.
5. _____ Chan is a serious student.
6. _____ He was a rug merchant.

a. drew plans for
b. thoughtful and quiet
c. piece of equipment
d. person who sells things
e. ~~musical beat~~
f. went out of sight
g. at a sharp angle

B. Complete each sentence. Use the Key Vocabulary words.

Example: I like to ski down ____steep____ hills.

1. The sound of that _____ has a steady _____.
2. Alice likes to _____ clothes for her friends.
3. The clothing _____ looked _____. He didn't smile.
4. When did your dog _____?

C. Choose three Key Vocabulary words and write a sentence using each one.

1. _____
2. _____
3. _____

Name _____ Date _____

● Reading Strategy
Compare and Contrast

Use with student book page 135.

> When you **compare** things, you see how they are **similar**. When you **contrast** items, you see how they are different.

Academic Vocabulary for the Reading Strategy	
Word	**Explanation**
compare	to look for ways that things are the same
contrast	to look for ways that things are different
similar	almost the same

A. Complete the sentences. Use a different Academic Vocabulary word in each sentence.

Example: Italian and Spanish are _____*similar*_____ languages.

1. People often _____ perfume and flowers because they smell alike.

2. It is easy to _____ life in a big city and life in a small town because they are so different.

3. A zebra is _____ to a horse.

B. Read the paragraph about Maria. Think about how you compare to and contrast with Maria. Then show if you are similar in the Venn diagram.

   Maria is 16 years old. She lives with her family, and she usually studies in the afternoon. Her favorite food is pasta. She likes to play outside, and she loves to ride her bike.

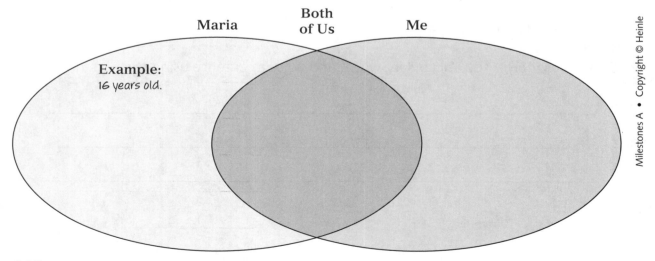

Maria   **Both of Us**   **Me**

Example:
16 years old.

Name _____ Date _____

● **Text Genre**

Use with student book page 136.

Play

Play	
cast of characters	the people in a play
dialogue	words characters say to one another
stage directions	words that tell the actors how to move and speak; these words are usually set in parentheses. For example: *(WINDRIDER enters from upstage.)*
scene	part of a play

Read the scene below.

Anna: *(Entering from stage right)* Oh, there you are!

Martin: Oh, hi, Anna. Were you looking for me?

Anna: Yes, I was. I need to talk to you.

Martin: *(Pause)* You do?

Anna: Yes. I want to talk about my party. I need your help.

Martin: I thought everything was all set.

Anna: *(Biting her lower lip)* Well, it was. But now there is a big problem.

Now read these parts from the scene. Identify each part as **character, dialogue,** or **stage direction.**

Example: *(Entering from stage right)*   _____stage direction_____

1. Martin   _____

2. Yes, I was. I need to talk to you.   _____

3. *(Pause)*   _____

4. Anna   _____

5. I thought everything was all set.   _____

6. *(Biting her lower lip)*   _____

Name _____   Date _____

● Reading Comprehension   *Use with student book page 143.*

Academic Vocabulary for the Reading Comprehension Questions	
Word	**Explanation**
inference	a guess based on some information
predict	to say what will happen in the future

A. Retell the story. Tell the main events of "Dragonwings." As you write, make inferences about what the characters are thinking and feeling.

_____

_____

_____

_____

B. Write your response. Do you enjoy reading stories about the past like "Dragonwings"? Why or why not?

_____

_____

_____

_____

_____

C. Assess the reading strategy. As you read "Dragonwings," you were asked to compare and contrast the characters. You also compared people's past and future lives. How did these comparisons help you understand the story? Choose a character and predict what he or she will do in the future.

_____

_____

_____

_____

_____

Milestones A • Copyright © Heinle

Name _____ Date _____

● Literary Element
Theme

Use with student book page 143.

> • A **theme** is an idea that is explored in literature.
> • A piece of literature can have more than one theme.
> • The author usually does not state the theme directly. The reader figures out the theme (or themes) while reading.

A. Read the story. Then check the sentence below that states the theme.

1 I was very excited when I got a job at the gym last year. I love to work out, and the gym let me work out for free. I was also excited about making money. I wanted to be able to take my friends out on the weekends.

2 I started in April. Everything was fine for a while. It was fun taking my friends to the movies, concerts, and other events. But then I noticed that sometimes they didn't seem so happy with me. One day Jerry said, "You always pay for everything. Do you think we don't have any money of our own?" Soon the guys stopped accepting my invitations.

3 The whole thing made me unhappy. I decided to have a serious talk with my friends. I apologized for making them upset. Then I told them I realized that I wasn't respecting them. I explained that I would pay my fair share when we went out, but I was not going to pay for everything all the time. In a few weeks, things were back to normal. And, in a few months, I had quite a bit in my bank account. I'd call it a win-win situation.

_____ 1.   Money always causes problems.

_____ 2.   Everyone should have a job.

_____ 3.   Money can cause problems between friends.

_____ 4.   Teenagers should not work and go to school.

_____ 5.   Everyone should save money.

B. What events and details in the story helped you identify the theme?

_____

_____

_____

Name _____ Date _____

● Vocabulary From the Reading

Use with student book page 144.

> **Key Vocabulary**
> engineer   invention
> experiment   modern

A. Rewrite the sentences using a Key Vocabulary word.

Example: New York is an up-to-date city.
　　　　　New York is a modern city.

1. Every day we do an activity in the chemistry laboratory.

　　_____

2. A scientist can design a bridge.

　　_____

3. Thomas Edison's lightbulb was an important solution to a problem.

　　_____

4. The Internet is a new creation.

　　_____

B. Match the sentence parts.

Example: __c__ Television was

1. _____ An engineer is

2. _____ The wheel is

3. _____ Young people usually have

4. _____ In ancient Greece, democracy was

a. a very old invention.

b. a new experiment.

c. ~~a 20th century invention.~~

d. modern ideas.

e. a special kind of scientist.

C. Complete the sentences. Use a different Key Vocabulary word in each item.

Example: Most ___modern___ homes have large windows, not small ones.

1. The _____ of the car caused a big demand for gasoline.

2. An _____ has to go to college.

3. We did an _____ to learn how much water plants need.

4. My parents do not like _____ music.

Name _____ Date _____

● Reading Strategy

Relate Your Own Experiences to a Reading

Use with student book page 145.

> As you read, **relate your own experiences to the reading.**

A. Look back at the passage on page 113 of this book. Then complete the chart below. List ways that the events and characters are similar to and different from those in your life.

Similar to My Life	Different from My Life
1. I like to buy things for friends.	1.
2.	2.
3.	3.

B. Think of another story that you have read in this book. Write the name of the story, and then complete the chart.

Title of the story: _____

Similar to My Life	Different from My Life

Name _____ Date _____

● Text Genre
Informational Text: Magazine Article

Use with student book page 145.

Magazine Article	
illustrations	art or photos that help the reader understand something described in the article
captions	short explanations of the illustrations

A. Match the title of each magazine with the type of illustrations it would contain.

Example: __d__ *Hollywood Today*

1. _____ *Automobile Weekly*

2. _____ *Financial News*

3. _____ *Fashion Times*

4. _____ *Scientific American*

5. _____ *Local Movie Guide*

a. A weekly calendar of information

b. Drawings of clothing

c. Photos of cars

d. ~~Photos of movie stars~~

e. Charts and graphs

f. Photos of modern inventions

B. Write a caption to go with each illustration below.

_____   _____   _____

C. Think of an important event in your life. Draw a picture about the event. Then write a caption to explain it.

```



```

Milestones A • Copyright © Heinle

Name _____ Date _____

● **Reading Comprehension** *Use with student book page 147.*

A. **Retell the story.** Describe the most important parts of "Da Vinci's Dreams" in your own words.

_____

_____

_____

_____

_____

_____

_____

B. **Write your response.** How did you react when you found out that Leonardo da Vinci designed things like the parachute and air-conditioning five hundred years ago?

_____

_____

_____

_____

_____

C. **Assess the reading strategy.** Relating your own experiences to a reading usually helps you understand the story better and enjoy it more. Why do you think this is true?

_____

_____

_____

_____

Name _____ Date _____

● Spelling

Use with student book page 147.

Titles Used with Names

When we speak or write to a person in a formal situation, we use a title before the person's name. It shows we respect the person.

Mr.	for any man	The store is owned by **Mr.** Smith.
Mrs.	for a married woman	**Mrs.** Soto is my history teacher.
Ms.	for any woman (but especially for an unmarried woman)	The librarian's name is **Ms.** Lin.
Miss	for an unmarried woman (Most people use *Ms.* instead.)	I live next door to **Miss** Applebee.
Dr.	for a medical doctor or someone who has a PhD degree	My dentist is **Dr.** Fujishige.
Prof.	for a professor at a college or university	**Prof.** Jacobs wrote a physics textbook.

A. Complete each sentence with the correct title. There may be more than one correct answer for some items.

Example: The man who drives the school bus is ____Mr.____ Chapin.

1. The woman doctor my mother goes to is _____ Martin.

2. The woman who works in the bakery is _____ Gonzalez.

3. My friend's mother is _____ Taylor.

4. My uncle is a professor at a college. His students call him _____ Han.

5. We call the man who delivers the mail _____ Ono.

6. My mother's unmarried friend is _____ Marino.

B. Write sentences about people you know using the titles in the chart.

Example: *Our landlady's name is Ms. Ackerman.*

1. _____

2. _____

3. _____

4. _____

Name _____ Date _____

● Writing Conventions

Use with student book page 147.

Punctuation: Commas in a Series

> When we list several items in a sentence, we place a **comma (,)** after each item. Some people leave out the final comma, the one before the word **and.** However, most writers prefer to use the final comma, and you should use it, too.

A. Rewrite the sentences. Add commas as necessary.

Example: _I am taking history, French, and physics._

1. I saw Larry Betty and Art at the movies last night.

   _____

2. Greed fear and anger are all negative emotions.

   _____

3. I went to the zoo the art museum and two stores this morning.

   _____

4. The weather was windy rainy and cold.

   _____

5. My uncle my aunt my grandmother and my cousin moved to Ohio.

   _____

B. Answer the following questions in full sentences. Include the final comma.

Example: What did you have for lunch?

   I had some spaghetti, some salad, and a glass of water.

1. What TV shows do you watch?

   _____

2. Who are your three best friends?

   _____

3. Which days do you have English class?

   _____

Name _____   Date _____

● Vocabulary Development
Use a Dictionary

Use with student book page 149.

A.   Here are two sentences from "Da Vinci's Dreams." Look at the underlined word in each one. Then look at the dictionary entry and answer the questions.

Sentence 1: Drawing the petals of a flower might give him the idea to create a new type of <u>gear</u>.

> **gear** /gɪr/ *n.* **1** a flat, round piece of metal with teeth around the edge that turns other gears in machinery: *The gears in my old clock need repair.* **2** one of several speeds in a vehicle: *I put the car into high gear and drove away.* **3** equipment, usually connected with sports: *The climber gathered up his gear and headed toward the mountain.*

Example: Does the word *gear* rhyme with *hair* or *here*?

   It rhymes with here.

1. What part of speech is **gear**?

   _____

2. Which meaning of **gear** is correct for this sentence?

   _____

Sentence 2: Leonardo also invented the first contact lenses, the monkey <u>wrench</u>, the diving snorkel, and the first parachute.

> **wrench** /rɛntʃ/ *n.* **wrenches 1** a metal tool that adjusts to tighten or loosen things: *He used a wrench to tighten the water pipes.* **2** a sudden twisting movement: *With one wrench, he loosened the cap off the jar.*
> —*v.* [T] **wrenches 1** to twist badly, hurt: *I fell and wrenched my back.* **2** to pull with a hard, twisting movement: *She had to wrench the door handle to open it.*

3. What two parts of speech can the word **wrench** be?

   _____

4. How many meanings are there for the noun **wrench**?

   _____

5. Which meaning of **wrench** is correct in this sentence?

   _____

Milestones A • Copyright © Heinle

Name _____ Date _____

● Grammar

Use with student book pages 150–151.

Conjunctions: *and, but*

The conjunction **and** connects two similar ideas. Note when a comma is needed.

words	He is wearing a hat **and** gloves.
phrases	Marta ate a sandwich **and** drank a glass of juice for lunch.
independent clauses	Leonardo designed inventions, **and** he made models to test his ideas.*

The conjunction **but** connects two contrasting ideas. Note when a comma is needed.

words	It is cold **but** sunny today.
independent clauses	Father had a few broken bones, **but** it was not serious.*

*When the conjunctions **and** or **but** connect two independent clauses, put a comma before the conjunction.

A. Underline all the independent clauses in these sentences. Sometimes there is only one. Circle the conjunctions.

Example: I like playing soccer, (but) I am better at basketball.

1. We got up early and left the house.

2. The bus was late, and I was upset.

3. The rain soon stopped, but we stayed home anyway.

4. I took my coat and my new red umbrella.

B. Combine the sentences. Use the word in parentheses. Use commas correctly.

Example: Moonshadow's father is in the U.S. His mother is in China. (but)

   Moonshadow's father is in the U.S., but his mother is in China.

1. Windrider tried to fly. It did not work. (but)

   _____

2. The wings separated. The wires broke. (and)

   _____

3. The airplane was wrecked. Windrider was hurt. (and)

   _____

Name _____ Date _____

C. Complete these sentences.

Example: I wanted to go swimming, but _the weather was too cold_ _____.

1. Chan likes to play soccer, but _____.

2. I do my homework in the afternoon, and _____.

3. It is three o'clock, and _____.

4. I am wearing a coat, but _____.

5. The room is large, and _____.

D. Combine sentences. Use **and** or **but**.

Example: He opened the door. He went inside.

He opened the door, and he went inside. _____

1. The food was expensive. It wasn't very good.

_____

2. Alan visited me in the hospital. He did not stay long.

_____

3. The dog barks. He does not bite.

_____

4. She closed the book. Then she put it on the shelf.

_____

5. I studied very hard. I got a great grade on the test.

_____

E. Complete these sentences with facts from your own life. Tell the truth.

Example: _I like tomatoes_ _____, but _I almost never eat them._ _____

1. _____, but _____.

2. _____, and _____.

3. _____, but _____.

4. _____, and _____.

5. _____, and _____.

Name _____ Date _____

● Grammar Expansion

Conjunction: *or*

The conjunction **or** gives a choice. Note when a comma is needed.

words	You can have soup for lunch **or** dinner.	no comma needed
phrases	He will eat at the fast-food place **or** Mac's Diner.	no comma needed
independent clauses	I may make a cake, **or** I may buy one at the store.	comma needed

A. Complete the sentences with the conjunction **or** or **and.**

Example: Do you want orange juice _____or_____ grapefruit juice with your lunch?

1. Is your birthday on Sunday _____ on Monday?

2. I want to go to the mall _____ do some shopping.

3. Is math difficult _____ easy for you?

4. Dictionaries give the pronunciation _____ the meaning of words.

5. You can sit, _____ you can stand.

6. We can eat at home, _____ we can go to a restaurant.

B. Complete the sentences with **or** plus a selection from the box.

a doctor / a businesswoman	he got up late / he missed his bus
go fishing / go to a ball game	~~scary movies / loud music~~
salad / soup	

Example: I do not like _scary movies or loud music_____.

1. What would you like for lunch, _____?

2. On Saturdays, my dad and I _____.

3. Alicia wants to be _____.

4. Tom is late. Probably _____.

Name _____ Date _____

C. Combine the sentences using **and, or,** or **but.** Use commas when necessary.

Example: Please open the window. Please turn on the air conditioner.

Please open the window or turn on the air conditioner.

1. We can eat at home. We can eat in a restaurant.

_____

2. I saw a movie about whales. I did not like it much.

_____

3. You can have water. You can have orange juice.

_____

4. First, I went to the movies. Later I had dinner.

_____

5. Today I am eating toast for breakfast. I usually have cereal.

_____

6. I can call you. You can call me.

_____

D. Complete each sentence with **and, but,** or **or.**

Example: I sometimes cook dinner, ____but____ it is not always very good.

1. I do my homework on my laptop _____ on my sister's computer.

2. I have a term paper _____ a book report due on Friday.

3. The term paper is finished, _____ I have not finished the book report yet.

4. I stayed home all day Saturday _____ Sunday.

5. I hope to get an A _____ a B on the term paper.

E. Describe pairs of activities that you sometimes do. Write sentences using the conjunctions **and, but,** and **or.**

Example: _On Saturdays I clean my room, but I do not do my homework._

1. _____

2. _____

3. _____

Name _____ Date _____

● Writing Assignment

Use with student book pages 152–153.

Expository Writing: Write a Compare and Contrast Paragraph

A. What was Windrider's dream? What is your dream for your future? Describe the two dreams here.

Windrider's Dream	My Dream
_____	_____
_____	_____
_____	_____
_____	_____
_____	_____
_____	_____
_____	_____
_____	_____

B. Use the Venn diagram below to show how your dream is similar to and different from Windrider's.

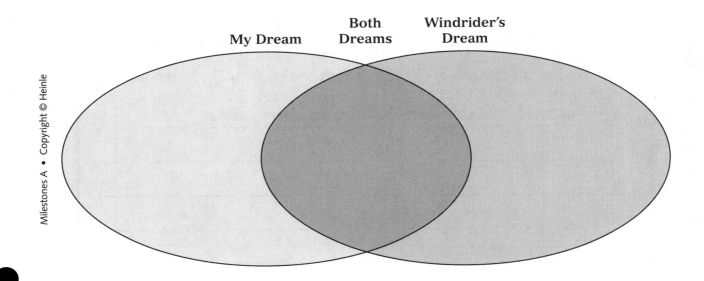

My Dream   Both Dreams   Windrider's Dream

Name _____ Date _____

● Writing Assignment
Writing Support

Use with student book page 153.

Grammar: Pronoun Referents

A **pronoun** is a word that takes the place of a noun. A **pronoun referent** is a pronoun that refers to a noun that has already been mentioned. Using pronoun referents makes your writing sound more natural.

A. Rewrite these sentences so that they sound more natural. Use pronoun referents.

Example: There are clouds in the sky, but I think the clouds will go away.

   There are clouds in the sky, but I think they will go away.

1. Maria studies a lot, but Maria hates taking tests.

   _____

2. You and I like music, and you and I both enjoy dancing.

   _____

3. The apartment is on the second floor, and the apartment is very light.

   _____

4. You and Tina can sleep late, but you and Tina should arrive by noon.

   _____

5. Take the spoons and forks, and put the spoons and forks on the table.

   _____

B. Write compound sentences about your friends and family using a pronoun referent in the second half.

Example: *Sami and Joe like to cook, but they hate doing dishes.*

1. _____

2. _____

3. _____

4. _____

Name _____ Date _____

● Writing Assignment
Revising Activity

Use with student book page 153.

A. Read the following paragraph. Mark the changes you need to make. Pay attention to these items:

> 1. Does the topic sentence state the main idea clearly?
> 2. Do all of the other sentences express clear and complete ideas?
> 3. Does the paragraph contain details and examples?
> 4. Does the conclusion summarize the main points?

    I have two brothers. My younger brother, Teddy, is very friendly. Teddy loves music. Teddy plays in a rock band and they practice. My older brother, Mike, is more serious. He studies a lot, and Mike does not like loud music. He is always asking Teddy to stop making so much noise. But Mike loves animals. I like Mike and Teddy.

B. Now rewrite the paragraph. Make changes and add sentences as necessary.

_____

_____

_____

_____

_____

_____

_____

_____

_____

_____

_____

_____

Name _____ Date _____

● Writing Assignment
Editing Activity

Use with student book page 153.

A. Read this compare and contrast paragraph and decide how to make it better. Use the editing marks on page 419 of your student book to mark changes. Pay attention to these items:

1. Indent the first sentence.
2. Begin each sentence with a capital letter.
3. Use some modals: **can, could, should,** and **must.**
4. Use the conjunctions **and** and **but** to combine words, phrases, and independent clauses.
5. Do not confuse **they're, their,** and **there.**

There are a lot of fun things about both summer sports and winter sports. In the summer you are outside all the time. You play tennis, go swimming. my friends always ride there bikes when it is not too hot. I love to exercise in the summer. I do not do it every day. sometimes I think people stay home and rest. In the winter people dress warmly for sports. They must be sure they are heads are covered. There hands must also stay warm. Skiing and snowboarding are fun. They can be dangerous. I prefer ice skating. you can still fall, but at least you are not going so fast. Both summer and winter sports are great.

B. Now rewrite the paragraph. Make the changes you marked above.

_____

_____

_____

_____

_____

_____

_____

_____

Name _____ Date _____

● Vocabulary From the Reading

Use with student book page 158.

> **Key Vocabulary**
>
> | | |
> |---|---|
> | honor | slave |
> | peace | violence |
> | segregation | wisdom |

A. Write the Key Vocabulary word that means the opposite of the phrases.

Example: all people mixed together ____*segregation*____

1. peacefulness _____

2. free person _____

3. shame _____

4. stupidity _____

5. war _____

B. Rewrite each sentence. Replace the underlined word with a Key Vocabulary word.

Example: A quiet forest is a place of <u>calmness</u>.

A quiet forest is a place of peace. _____

1. The more we learn, the more <u>understanding</u> we have.

_____

2. Putting cats and dogs in the same room can cause <u>trouble</u>.

_____

3. Putting boys and girls in separate classes is an example of <u>separation</u>.

_____

C. Use the Key Vocabulary words in three sentences. Use the sentences to state your opinion about different issues.

Example: ____*Violence doesn't solve problems.*____

1. _____

2. _____

3. _____

Name _____   Date _____

● **Reading Strategy**   *Use with student book page 159.*

Distinguish Fact from Opinion

> A **fact** is a piece of information that is true. An **opinion** is something that someone thinks or believes. As you read, you can use **evidence** in the text to **distinguish** between fact and opinion.

Academic Vocabulary for the Reading Strategy	
Word	**Explanation**
distinguish	to see or understand how things are different
evidence	words or things that show something is true

A. Read the following sentences. Write the letter that tells what the person is doing. **D** = distinguishing between two things; **G** = giving evidence

Example: __*G*__ I opened my wallet to show I didn't have any money.

1. _____ Carlos is a little taller than Roberto.

2. _____ I showed my report card to my parents.

3. _____ Emma showed that her hands were clean.

4. _____ I like tacos better than pizza.

B. Read the following sentences. Label each one **fact** or **opinion**.

Example: _____*opinion*_____ The weather is nice today.

1. _____ The temperature is 70 degrees.

2. _____ I rode my bicycle to school today.

3. _____ That movie was really interesting.

4. _____ The movie tickets cost $10.

5. _____ Carla has a beautiful voice.

6. _____ Carla has over 100 CDs at her house.

Name _____ Date _____

● Text Genre

Informational Text

Use with student book page 160.

Informational Text	
facts	information that can be proven
headings	titles used for separate sections of the text, usually in large bold type
captions	words that explain a picture

Read the passage.

Tamim Ansary

Early Life in Afghanistan

Tamim Ansary was born in 1948. His father was a science teacher at Kabul University. His mother taught English at a girls' school in Afghanistan. Later the family went to live in a small town called Lashkargah in the middle of the desert.

Life in the United States

At the age of 16, Ansary won a scholarship and was able to attend high school in Colorado. After that, he went to Reed College and graduated with honors. After graduation, he worked in restaurants, traveled a lot, and began his writing career. He now lives in San Francisco.

Complete the chart.

Features of the Text	Examples from the Text
1. Facts—List one fact about his family, one about his education, and one about a job he had.	Tamim Ansary was born in 1948.
2. Headings	_____ _____
3. Caption	_____

Name _____ Date _____

● Reading Comprehension

Use with student book page 167.

Academic Vocabulary for the Reading Comprehension Questions	
Word	**Explanation**
affect	to change, to have an impact on
support	to hold up, to keep from falling or slipping

A. Retell the story. Retell part of Tamim Ansary's story "Martin Luther King Jr. Day." Include at least two facts and two opinions in your paragraph.

_____

_____

_____

_____

_____

_____

B. Write your response. Choose one opinion you found in the reading about Dr. Martin Luther King Jr. and give evidence from the reading to support this opinion.

_____

_____

_____

_____

C. Assess the reading strategy. How does being able to distinguish facts from opinions affect your understanding of the story?

_____

_____

_____

_____

Milestones A • Copyright © Heinle

Name _____ Date _____

● **Text Element**

Use with student book page 167.

Chronological Order

> Many informational texts present information in chronological order. These texts
> include dates and signal words. Signal words give the reader information about the
> order of events. Some signal words are: **before, during, after, then.**

A. Read the paragraph below. Then number the events in the order they happened.

Last Saturday, Kenji decided to have a party. He wanted to invite a lot of people.
But before he invited anyone, he checked with his parents. They said it was fine
with them. It was going to be expensive so he decided to invite only a few people.
After everyone arrived, he was glad he hadn't invited any more people. The party
was great and everyone had fun. Before they left, his friends helped him clean up.

_____ Kenji checked with his parents.

_____ He was glad he hadn't invited any more people.

_____ Kenji decided to invite only a few people.

_____ The party was great.

___1___ Kenji decided to have a party.

_____ Kenji's friends helped him clean up.

B. Read the following paragraph. Then number the events in the order they
happened.

On Wednesday, Carol studied hard for a test. She studied after school. She
also studied a lot after dinner. She was very tired when she stopped studying.
When she went to bed, she couldn't stop thinking about the test. She didn't sleep
well. On Thursday morning, she didn't feel well. The test was at 10:00. She did
her best, but she was a little worried. On Friday morning, the teacher gave her
test back to her. She got a B+. Carol was happy, but she wanted to do better the
next time. She realized that she needed to sleep well before taking a test.

_____ She was a little worried.

_____ On Friday, she got the test back.

_____ She went to bed.

___1___ Carol studied hard for a test after school.

_____ She got a B+.

_____ She took the test on Thursday at 10:00.

_____ She studied after dinner.

Name _____ Date _____

● **Vocabulary From the Reading**   *Use with student book page 168.*

Key Vocabulary	
frozen	stuck
hope	

A.   Write the Key Vocabulary word for each definition.

Word	Definition
Example: ____*frozen*____	as cold as ice
1. _____	to want something to happen
2. _____	attached, as with tape or glue
3. _____	changed from a liquid into a solid state

B.   Complete each sentence. Use one of the Key Vocabulary words in your answer.

Example: Are you sure the rain will stop soon?

I'm not sure, but that's what I ____*hope*____.

1. Why did you come home so early?

The wind was really cold and my face was _____.

2. How did he hang that picture?

He _____ it to the wall with tape.

3. Will you get an A on the test?

I _____ so.

4. Can you open that window?

No, I can't. It's _____.

5. Can we go skating tonight?

Yes, the lake is _____.

C.   Write three sentences, each with a Key Vocabulary word in it.

1. _____

2. _____

3. _____

134

Name _____ Date _____

● Reading Strategy
Identify Repetition in Poetry

Use with student book page 169.

> **Repetition** is saying or writing something more than once.

A. Read the following poem.

> The fire truck leaves the station near my house
> Speeding, screaming through the empty streets.
> I awake with a start, the noise
> Speeding, screaming through my ears.

1. Which phrase is repeated?

   _____

2. Why do you think it is repeated?

   _____

   _____

   _____

B. Now read this poem.

> Excited, Ronnie's picking out a puppy
> Excited, the puppy's picking out Ronnie.
> Excited, they jump into the back seat.
> Excited, they run around the house at home.

1. Which word is repeated several times?

   _____

2. Why do you think it is repeated?

   _____

   _____

   _____

Name _____   Date _____

● Text Genre

Use with student book page 169.

Poetry

Poetry	
stanzas	groups of lines
rhyme	words having the same ending sound
sensory language	words that help you see, hear, smell, touch, and taste what the poet is describing
rhythm	a regular beat

A. Write **T** for **true** statements and **F** for **false** statements.

Example: __F__ Two inches long is an example of sensory language.

1. _____ Most music has a regular rhythm.

2. _____ A stanza must be one line long.

3. _____ The words **sky blue eyes** contain sensory language.

4. _____ Words that rhyme have all the same letters.

5. _____ A drum can make rhymes.

6. _____ A poem can contain more than one stanza.

B. Choose the best word to complete these statements about poetry. Write **a**, **b**, or **c** as your answer.

__b__ Example: A poem with four beats to every line has a regular

        a. sensory language.   b. rhythm.   c. rhyme.

_____ 1. An example of sensory language includes the word

        a. first.   b. warm.   c. expensive.

_____ 2. The words **sing** and **ring** make a

        a. rhyme.   b. rhythm.   c. stanza.

_____ 3. A **stanza** is like a

        a. sentence.   b. paragraph.   c. line.

_____ 4. The words **soft** and **smooth** are an example of

        a. a rhyme.   b. a stanza.   c. sensory language.

Name _____ Date _____

● Reading Comprehension   *Use with student book page 173.*

A. Get meaning from poetry. What are the poems "Dreams," "The Dream on my Wall," and "The Student Teacher" about?

_____

_____

_____

_____

_____

_____

_____

B. Write your response. How did the repetition in the poems in this unit affect your understanding of them?

_____

_____

_____

_____

C. Assess the reading strategy. Do you think that repeating words and phrases adds something important to a poem? Why or why not?

_____

_____

_____

_____

Name _____ Date _____

● Spelling

Use with student page 173.

Abbreviations in Names

An **abbreviation** is a single letter that represents a word. It is always followed by a period.

1. Abbreviations that tell more about a person and come after the person's name are always followed by a period.
   - Dr. Martin Luther King **Jr.** (His father had the same name.)
   - Ms. Joan Sillins, **M.A.** (She has a Master of Arts degree.)
   - Jacob Wilson, **M.D.** (He is a medical doctor.)
   - David Gilroy, **D.D.S.** (He's a dentist.)

2. The abbreviation for a part of a person's name is always followed by a period.
   - Dr. **M. L.** King Jr.
   - Robert **E.** Lee
   - **K. D.** Lang

A. Write the person's name using an abbreviation.

Example: My father, Gary Lima, is a medical doctor. _Dr. Gary Lima, M.D._

1. My mother, Raquel Soto, has a Master of Arts degree. _____

2. My uncle, Harry Black, is a dentist. _____

3. My friend has the same name as his father, Freddy Cook. _____

B. Rewrite the sentences with the correct abbreviations.

Example: The teacher's name is Ms. Mary L Mack, MA.
   The teacher's name is Ms. Mary L. Mack, M.A.

1. Mr Robert F Kreskin jr is my uncle.

   _____

2. The singer's name is G G Gordon.

   _____

3. I met Dr Gilbert Nachman, PhD

   _____

4. Her name is Dr. Sarah F Bloom, MD.

   _____

Milestones A • Copyright © Heinle

Name _____ Date _____

● **Writing Conventions**

Use with student book page 173.

Punctuation: Commas in Addresses

> We use commas to separate the various parts of place names and addresses.
> 1. Use a comma to separate the name of a city and a state.
>   Los Angeles, California
>
> 2. Use a comma to separate a street address or post office box from a city name.
>   23 Lincoln Avenue, Springfield, Missouri
>   P.O. Box 42, Albany, New York
>
> 3. Do not use a comma to separate a street number from a street name
>   **Correct:** 450 Main Street, Elba, New York
>   **Incorrect:** 450, Main Street, Elba, New York
>
> 4. Do not use a comma to separate a zip code from a state name.
>   **Correct:** Chicago, Illinois 60660
>   **Incorrect:** Chicago, Illinois, 60660

A. Rewrite the following addresses correctly.

Example: 67 Center Street Baylor Kentucky

67 Center Street, Baylor, Kentucky _____

1. 1040 Fifth, Avenue New York New York

_____

2. P.O. Box 1472 Berkeley California, 94707

_____

3. 4500, West Ninth Street Milwaukee Wisconsin 53202

_____

4. 35 Ocean Drive Miami Florida, 33015

_____

5. 59, Farview Farm, Road, Connecticut, 06896

_____

6. P,O, Box 12428, Austin Texas, 78711

_____

Name _____   Date _____

● Vocabulary Development

Use with student book page 175.

Multiple-Meaning Words

> **Multiple-meaning words** are two or more words that are pronounced the same and often spelled the same.

A. Match each word with its two correct meanings.

Example: __i__ __j__ **change**

1. ____ ____ **watch**

2. ____ ____ **bank**

3. ____ ____ **play**

4. ____ ____ **light**

a. the opposite of heavy

b. to have fun doing something

c. the ground beside a river

d. the opposite of darkness

e. something that tells you the time

f. a safe place to put money

g. to use your eyes to see something

h. participate in a sport

i. coins

j. to make something different

B. Complete the sentence with the correct multiple-meaning word from Exercise A.

Example: The students went to the park to __play__.

1. The fishermen sat on the _____ of a small stream.

2. My new laptop computer is very _____.

3. Did you _____ television last night?

4. Do you know how to _____ tennis?

C. Write four sentences or your own, each with one of the multiple-meaning words above.

1. _____

2. _____

3. _____

4. _____

Name _____ Date _____

● Grammar

Use with student book pages 176–177.

Modals: *can, could, should, must*

Modal	Use to …	Example
can	talk about ability in the present	I am 18. I **can** vote this year.
could	talk about ability in the past	I was 17 last year. I **could** not vote last year.
should	give advice and suggestions	You look sick. You **should** go to the doctor.
must	talk about something that is necessary or required	Cars **must** stop at red lights.

A. What does the modal in each sentence do? Choose the correct answer.

____d____ **Example:** Ellen can speak four languages.
   a. It says that something is necessary.
   b. It gives advice.
   c. It talks about past ability.
   d. It talks about present ability.

_____ 1. Tom should get more exercise.
   a. It says that something is necessary.
   b. It gives advice.
   c. It talks about past ability.
   d. It talks about present ability.

_____ 2. We must leave before 8:00.
   a. It says that something is necessary.
   b. It gives advice.
   c. It talks about past ability.
   d. It talks about present ability.

_____ 3. Howard can name all 50 state capitals.
   a. It says that something is necessary.
   b. It gives advice.
   c. It talks about past ability.
   d. It talks about present ability.

_____ 4. At the age of six months, I could already walk.
   a. It says that something is necessary.
   b. It gives advice.
   c. It talks about past ability.
   d. It talks about present ability.

Name _____   Date _____

● Grammar Expansion

Positive and Negative Modals

Modals: Positive			
subject	**modal**	**base form of verb**	**object**
John	should	do	his homework.

Modals: Negative				
subject	**modal**	**not**	**base form of verb**	**object**
John	should	not	forget	his book.

Note: The negative of **can** is **cannot**.

A. Complete each sentence with the correct modal.

Example: We __must__ be quiet in the library.

1. I _____ ride a little bicycle when I was three years old.

2. It's not necessary, but you _____ try to arrive 15 minutes early.

3. It's not raining today, so we _____ go swimming.

4. You _____ pay for anything you take from a store.

B. Rewrite the sentences. Use the negative forms of the modals.

Example: We should watch TV all day.
   We should not watch TV all day.

1. Dr. King said people should meet hate with hate.

   _____

2. Dr. King said the U.S. must remain a divided country.

   _____

3. Mr. North can fix his car.

   _____

4. Miss Moreno could speak English when she came from El Salvador.

   _____

Name _____ Date _____

● Grammar Expansion
Question Modals

Modals: Questions			
modal	subject	base form of verb	object
Can	she	play	the piano well?
Could	you	understand	algebra ten years ago?
Should	I	do	my homework now?

Note: We rarely use **must** in questions. We usually say **Do we have to** go now? or **Does he have to** buy a new book? See page 144.

Rewrite these sentences in question form.

Example: They could swim every day when we lived near the beach.
Could they swim every day when they lived near the beach?

1. A student teacher can teach a class.

    _____

2. We should ask for help.

    _____

3. Alan could talk when he was one year old.

    _____

4. Yoko should take a vacation.

    _____

5. Susana can help us with our project.

    _____

6. The city should provide better transportation.

    _____

7. I can eat dinner now.

    _____

8. He should go to the office right now.

    _____

Name _____ Date _____

● Grammar Expansion
Modal: *must*

> The modal **must** has two meanings. The meaning you saw on page 141 shows that something is necessary or required.
>   We **must** wear sneakers in the gymnasium.
>
> Another meaning of **must** is to show that something is probably true.
>   Rosa grew up in Mexico. She **must** speak Spanish.

A. How is the modal **must** used in these sentences? Write **necessary** or **probably** in front of each sentence.

Example: ___*necessary*___ The door is locked. You must ask for the key.

1. _____ You ordered the food. You must pay for it.

2. _____ Melba bought a new car. She must have a lot of money.

3. _____ The students are standing outside. Class must be over.

4. _____ It is raining. You must take your umbrella.

5. _____ Carla isn't in class. She must be sick.

B. Read each sentence and write a sentence of your own using **must** to express something that is probably true.

Example: Selena isn't in school today.
    She must be sick.

1. Tom worked on his project until midnight last night.

   _____

2. Jasmine's cat ran away yesterday, but today it came back.

   _____

3. Felipe took all of his friends to the movies yesterday.

   _____

4. I got a very good grade on my science test.

   _____

5. Miguel didn't wear his jacket today, and the weather was very cold.

   _____

Name _____ Date _____

● Writing Assignment

Use with student book pages 178–179.

Persuasive Essay: Nominate a Person to Honor

A. Paragraph 1

Describe the type of person who deserves to be nominated. Give the person's name.

Example: Type of Person: *Someone who helped other people*

Name: *Princess Diana*

Type of person: _____

Name: _____

B. Paragraph 2

Give facts, details, and examples that convince the reader to agree with you. You can use the Internet, an encyclopedia, or library books to gather more information.

Example: Reason: *Princess Diana helped poor people around the world.*

Fact: *She was vice president of the British Red Cross.*

Detail: *In 1997, she visited Bosnia to help children there.*

Reasons: _____

_____

Facts: _____

_____

Details: _____

_____

C. Paragraph 3

Restate your nomination and summarize your reasons.

Reasons: _____

_____

Name _____ Date _____

● Writing Assignment

Use with student book page 179.

Writing Support

> **Spelling: Commonly Confused Words**
> Some words sound the same but have different meanings and different spellings.
>
> **their** = possessive pronoun They wrote **their** essays.
> **there** = a place My class is **there**.
> **they're** = contraction for **they are** **They're** working together.

A. Complete the sentences with **their, there,** or **they're**.

Example: They forgot _____their_____ money so they couldn't buy anything.

1. Put your books over _____ on the table.

2. My parents are in _____ room.

3. _____ watching TV right now.

4. It isn't here. It's _____.

5. The children aren't sleeping. _____ playing outside.

6. Look at that tall building _____ on the corner.

7. The teachers enjoy _____ vacations a lot.

8. The Bakers are taking _____ children to the zoo.

9. I forgot my running shoes. _____ under my bed at home.

10. _____ my favorite running shoes.

B. Complete these sentences. Tell about your own life.

Example: __My friends dropped__ their __coats on the floor__.

1. _____ there.

2. _____. They're _____.

3. _____ their _____.

Name _____ Date _____

● Writing Assignment
Revising Activity

Use with student book page 179.

Study each revision tip for a persuasive essay. Then read each sentence and fill in the second column. You can make up (imagine) the facts, details, and examples.

Revision Tip # 1: Use facts to make your argument more convincing.

First Sentence	Follow-up Fact
Ramon Perez is a great runner.	He has competed in the Olympics twice.
Lee Ho Sook is a talented writer.	
David Baker has helped a lot of people.	
Carol Traymor is an excellent cook.	

Revision Tip # 2: Use examples and details to make your argument more convincing.

First Sentence	Follow-up Example or Detail
Ramon Perez has won a lot of races.	
Lee Ho Sook has written many books.	
David Baker started a foundation.	
Carol Traymor has some famous friends.	

Name _____ Date _____

● Writing Assignment
Editing Activity

Use with student book page 179.

A. Read this paragraph from a persuasive essay and decide how to make it better. Use the editing marks on page 419 of your student book to mark changes. Pay attention to these items:

1. Indent the first sentence.
2. Begin each sentence with a capital letter.
3. Use the conjunctions **and** and **but** to combine sentences.
4. Don't confuse **they're, their,** and **there**.
5. Use pronoun referents correctly.

Stephen Spielberg is one of the greatest film makers of our time. his movies appeal to all ages and types of people. He has made children's movies like Hook. He has made historical dramas like Munich. He has made several science fiction movies including ET and War of the Worlds. He makes a lot of movies and there almost always successful. When E.T. the Extra Terrestrial came out in 1982, they became the highest-earning movie ever. Spielberg is also known for the high quality of its work. He has won several Academy Awards including Best Director and Best picture for Jurassic Park in 1993.

B. Now rewrite the paragraph. Make the changes you marked above.

_____

_____

_____

_____

_____

_____

_____

_____

_____

Name _____   Date _____

● **Vocabulary From the Reading**   *Use with student book page 196.*

Key Vocabulary

apology	refugee
comfort	safe
grateful	trust

A. Write the Key Vocabulary word for each definition.

Word	Definition
Example: _____*trust*_____	have confidence in someone or something
1. _____	a person leaving behind bad living conditions
2. _____	thankful
3. _____	what you say when you are sorry for doing something wrong
4. _____	ease someone's pain or worry
5. _____	not in danger

B. Circle the correct word in each sentence.

Example: I feel (safe /(grateful)) for all the good friends I have.

1. The new (apology / refugee) did not have anywhere to live.

2. That old bridge does not look (grateful / safe).

3. I accepted his (apology / refugee) for forgetting our date.

4. She tried to (trust / comfort) the baby so it would stop crying.

C. Answer the questions. Use a Key Vocabulary word in each answer.

Example: Would you ride your bike in a big city?

    No, I do not think that is a safe thing to do.

1. Can you depend on your friends?

_____

2. What are you thankful for?

_____

3. What do you call a man who has to leave his country?

_____

Name _____ Date _____

● Reading Strategy

Use with student book page 197.

Identify Cause and Effect

When one event makes another one happen, it is called **cause and effect**.

Academic Vocabulary for the Reading Strategy	
Word	**Explanation**
cause	a reason why something happens
effect	a result

Read the sentences. Then complete the chart.

Example: Because it was raining, I took my umbrella.

Cause	Effect
It was raining. ⟶	I took my umbrella.

1. Alan was bored. He left early.

Cause	Effect
⟶	

2. I was tired. I went to bed early.

Cause	Effect
⟶	

3. We jumped up when we heard the loud noise.

Cause	Effect
⟶	

4. We took a taxi because it was raining.

Cause	Effect
⟶	

Milestones A • Copyright © Heinle

Name _____ Date _____

● Text Genre
Historical Fiction

Use with student book page 198.

Historical Fiction	
setting	the story is set in a real place and time
characters	the characters may be made-up or imaginary; some may also be real people
plot	the plot is a combination of fictional events and events that really happened

Read the story. Then label the sentences listed below it. Use the words **setting, character,** and **plot.**

(Example) The tiny cabin sits in the middle of a flat, brown field outside of Hodgenville, Kentucky. (1) There are no trees anywhere around, nothing green as far as the eye can see. (2) We see a tall, thin man opening the door and stepping outside. (3) He looks around, shakes his head, and then stares at the ground. (4) The year is 1809. (5) The man does not realize it, but he has just become the father of the man who will be the sixteenth president of the United States, Abraham Lincoln.

(6) Three years later, the Lincoln family moves to a farm in another part of Hodgenville. (7) When he is six, Abe starts attending school. (8) The school looks a lot like the cabin he lives in. (9) It is built of logs and has only one room. Abe's sister, Sarah, is two years older. She and Abe attend the same school. (10) The children's mother suddenly dies when Abe is only nine years old.

Example: _____ setting _____

Sentence 1 _____   Sentence 6 _____

Sentence 2 _____   Sentence 7 _____

Sentence 3 _____   Sentence 8 _____

Sentence 4 _____   Sentence 9 _____

Sentence 5 _____   Sentence 10 _____

Name _____ Date _____

● Reading Comprehension

Use with student book page 209.

Academic Vocabulary for the Reading Comprehension Questions	
Word	**Explanation**
examine	to look at closely
develop	to turn into something more complete, greater, better, or bigger

A. **Retell the story.** Include some examples of cause and effect from "Suzy and Leah."

_____

_____

_____

_____

B. **Write your response.** What did you learn from the story? Think of a time when you misunderstood another person, or when another person misunderstood you. Examine this misunderstanding and then tell about it.

_____

_____

_____

_____

C. **Assess the reading strategy.** As you read "Suzy and Leah," you were asked to look for examples of cause and effect. How did studying these examples help you develop your understanding the story?

_____

_____

_____

_____

Name _____ Date _____

● Literary Elements

Use with student book page 209.

Plot, Conflict, Climax, and Resolution

> **plot**
> The sequence of events in a story is called the **plot**. A plot usually has a beginning, a middle, and an end. It also usually includes a conflict and a resolution.

> **conflict and climax**
> Most plots include a **conflict**. A conflict is a problem or struggle at the center of the story.
> The conflict often grows to an exciting or high point when things start to change. This is called the **climax**.

> **resolution**
> The end of a story usually shows the **resolution** of the conflict. The resolution is how the conflict is resolved.

Each item below contains three key points in a short story. Match each sentence with the correct literary element.

A.

Example: ___*a*___ Ron is the shortest boy on the basketball team. The other boys sometimes make fun of him.

   a. conflict

   b. climax

   c. resolution

1. _____ One day, Ron scores the winning point at an important game.

2. _____ The other team members carry him off on their shoulders. They tell Ron that they are happy he is on their team.

B.

1. _____ Linda borrows her sister's computer and finishes the assignment on time.

   a. conflict

   b. climax

   c. resolution

2. _____ Linda is typing her term paper, which is due tomorrow morning, but she is not sure she can finish it on time.

3. _____ Suddenly, Linda's computer crashes and she gets upset.

Name _____ Date _____

● Vocabulary From the Reading

Use with student book page 210.

Key Vocabulary

advice	compromise
annoy	misunderstanding
blame	upset

A. Write the Key Vocabulary word for each definition.

Word	Definition
Example: ____advice____	an opinion about what someone should do
1. _____	come to an agreement where two people each give up something
2. _____	disturb; worry
3. _____	make someone a little angry
4. _____	confusion; lack of clear understanding
5. _____	say that someone is responsible for something wrong

B. Complete each sentence. Use one of the Key Vocabulary words.

Example: My brother and I had a ___misunderstanding___ about money.

1. Let me give you some good _____ about learning English.

2. They will _____ to watch a movie they both like.

3. We should not _____ the coach if the team loses.

4. Losing this watch would _____ me greatly.

5. Does the sound of chalk on the blackboard _____ you?

C. Tell about how you felt when you had a disagreement with a friend. What did you do about the disagreement? Use as many of the Key Vocabulary words as you can.

_____

_____

_____

Milestones A • Copyright © Heinle

Name _____ Date _____

Use with student book page 211.

● Reading Strategy
Identify Cause and Effect

> When one event makes another one happen, it is called **cause and effect**.

Look back at the two situations on page 153 in this book. Then complete the cause-and-effect charts for each situation.

Situation #1

Example:		
Cause		**Effect**
Ron is the shortest boy on the basketball team.	⟶	The other boys make fun of him.
1. _____ _____ _____ _____	⟶	_____ _____ _____ _____

Situation #2

Example:		
Cause		**Effect**
1. _____ _____ _____ _____	⟶	_____ _____ _____ _____
2. _____ _____ _____ _____	⟶	_____ _____ _____ _____

Name _____ Date _____

● Text Genre
Informational Text

Use with student book page 211.

Informational Text	
subject	what the text is about
headings	titles that tell you what a part of the text is about
definitions	meanings of new words

Read the informational text below. Notice the words that have definitions within the reading passage. Then complete the chart.

Avoiding Conflicts

1 The best way to create good feelings among friends and classmates is to learn to avoid conflicts. You can have strong opinions, but you have to learn to respect other people's opinions. You show that you value their opinions even if you do not agree. Also, you do not gossip, which means to talk about people in a negative way.

Learning to Calm Down

2 A friend may say something that makes you upset or causes a strong reaction. You may want to make a quick retort, that is, an angry response, but this usually leads to further conflict. Try taking a deep breath to calm down. Then continue the discussion in a respectful way. Then you may find a resolution to the conflict.

Feature	Examples from the Text
subject of the readings	_____
headings	(Paragraph 1) _____ (Paragraph 2) _____
definitions	(Paragraph 1) Word: **respect** Definition: _____ _____ (Paragraph 2) Word: **retort** Definition: _____ _____

Milestones A • Copyright © Heinle

Name _____ Date _____

● **Reading Comprehension**   *Use with student book page 215.*

A.   Summarize the reading. Think back to *The Kids' Guide to Working Out Conflicts.* Write about some of the things you can do when a conflict develops.

_____

_____

_____

_____

_____

_____

B.   Write your response. Did this reading cause you to examine your own behavior? If so, what things might you want to do differently when you get in a conflict?

_____

_____

_____

_____

C.   Assess the reading strategy. As you read *The Kid's Guide to Working Out Conflicts*, you were asked to identify examples of cause and effect. How did identifying these examples help you understand the story?

_____

_____

_____

_____

Name _____ Date _____

● **Spelling**   *Use with student book page 215.*

Full Forms and Abbreviations of Days and Months

We often abbreviate the words for the days of the week and the months of the year.
1. These abbreviations are always followed by a period.
2. They usually include the first three letters of the name of the day or month.

Days of the Week							
Full Forms	Sunday	Monday	Tuesday	Wednesday	Thursday	Friday	Saturday
Abbreviations	Sun.	Mon.	Tues. Tue.	Wed.	Thurs. Thur.	Fri.	Sat.

Months of the Year						
Full Forms	January	February	March	April	May	June
Abbreviations	Jan.	Feb.	Mar.	Apr.	(no abbreviation)	Jun.
Full Forms	July	August	September	October	November	December
Abbreviations	Jul.	Aug.	Sept.	Oct.	Nov.	Dec.

A. Rewrite these dates using the full forms. Use a comma between the day and the month.

Example: Mon. Oct 14 <u>Monday, October 14</u>

1. Wed. Jan. 17 _____ 4. Tues. Apr. 1 _____

2. Sat. Aug. 11 _____ 5. Thurs. Mar. 13 _____

3. Sun. Dec. 20 _____ 6. Mon. Jul. 4 _____

B. Write the following dates using abbreviations for the day and month.

Example: When were you born? <u>Tues, Aug. 12, 1998</u>

1. What is today's date? _____

2. When did school open this year? _____

3. When will school end this year? _____

4. What was the first day of this year? _____

Milestones A • Copyright © Heinle

Name _____ Date _____

● Writing Conventions

Use with student book page 215.

Punctuation: Cited Sources

Follow these guidelines when you cite, or list, your sources for a research report.

Book	Author's name, last name first + period Full title, underlined + period City where the book was published + colon Name of publisher + comma Date the book was published + period

Kostman, Joel. <u>Keys to the City.</u> New York: DK Publishing, Inc., 1997.

Encyclopedia	Title of the article in quotation marks + period Name of the encyclopedia underlined + period The year the encyclopedia was published + period

"Northwest Passage." <u>World Book Encyclopedia.</u> 1998.

Web Site	Title of the article in quotation marks + period Title of the Web site underlined + period Web site address with angled brackets around it

"Space Food." <u>NASA Quest.</u> <http://spaceflight.nasa.gov/living/spacefood/>

Cite these sources correctly. Follow the guidelines above.

Example: A company called the Globe Pequot Press in Guilford, Connecticut, published a book called *Eating Right* in 2004. The author is Jane Stevens.

Stevens, Jane. <u>Eating Right.</u> Guilford: Globe Pequot Press, 2004.

1. I used a Web site called Time to Read. The address is http://readingtime.org. The title of the article was "A Daily Reading Log."

   _____

   _____

2. I used a book called *Moon Rocks,* which was published by Green Press in 2006. The company is located in Philadelphia. The author was Ronald Rice.

   _____

   _____

Name _____ Date _____

● Vocabulary Development

Use with student book page 217.

Use Figurative Language

> Figurative language describes something by comparing it to something else. Authors use figurative language to give the reader a new way of looking at something. Here are some similes:
>
> My room is like a jungle.
> She runs like the wind.

A. Match each sentence starter with the correct ending.

Example: ___*e*___ His smile was like

1. _____ The dress was all pink and gold   a. like a tired elephant.

2. _____ The kitten was crying   b. like a punch in the stomach.

3. _____ His angry words hit me   c. like a sunset.

4. _____ The cold rain felt   d. like a baby.

5. _____ He walked slowly up the stairs   e. ~~a bright summer day.~~

                                                 f. like an icy shower.

B. Use similes to describe these people, places, and things.

Example: A friend
          Susan is like a bulldog. She never gives up.

1. Your house

_____

2. Your notebook

_____

3. Your guardian

_____

Name _____ Date _____

● Grammar
The Future Tense: *will*

Use with student book page 218.

The Future Tense with *will*			
Subject	*Will*	*(Not)*	**Base Verb**
I			
He / She / It	**will**	**(not)**	try.
You / We / They			

A. Rewrite the sentences. Use the negative form of **will.**

Example: Little Avi will speak to people.
Little Avi will not speak to people.

1. Leah and Suzy will speak to each other.

   _____

2. Leah will wear her name tag.

   _____

3. Leah will take her notebook back to the shelter.

   _____

4. Leah will tell the doctors she is ill.

   _____

B. Complete the sentences with **will** or **will not** to make predictions.

Example: I ____will____ graduate from college.

1. I _____ get married.

2. I _____ have children.

3. Doctors _____ find a cure for cancer next year.

4. People _____ travel to Mars in ten years.

5. The world _____ be a peaceful place in twenty years.

Name _____ Date _____

● Grammar

The Future Tense: *be going to*

Use with student book page 219.

The Future Tense with *be going to*				
subject	*be*	*(not)*	*going to*	base verb
I	am			
He / She / It	is	(not)	going to	leave.
You / We / They	are			

A. Use the words to write sentences with **be going to**.

Example: (is / he / to / have / fight / a / going)

    <u>He is going to have a fight.</u>

1. (conflict / grow / going / is / the / to)

    _____

2. (going / am / be / conflict solver / I / to / a)

    _____

3. (smart / act / going / am / to / I)

    _____

4. (avoid / are / going / we / physical fights / to)

    _____

B. Change these sentences to their negative form.

Example: I am going to use put-downs.

    <u>I am not going to use put-downs.</u>

1. She is going to blame the other person.

    _____

2. They are going to try to win the argument.

    _____

3. He is going to take sides.

    _____

4. We are going to gossip.

    _____

Name _____ Date _____

● Grammar Expansion
Future Tense Questions with *will* and *be going to*

Future Tense Questions with *will*			
will	subject	base verb	
Will	I he / she / it you / we / they	*win*	the game?

Future Tense Questions with *be going to*				
be	subject	*going to*	base verb	
Am	I			
Is	he / she / it	**going to**	win	the game?
Are	you / we / they			

A. Use the words to write questions with **will**.

Example: (involved / you / get / will / in gossip)
　　　　　　 Will you get involved in gossip?

1. (you / in their place / yourself / put / will)

　　_____

2. (listen / will / the other person / you / to)

　　_____

3. (it / will / sunny / be / tomorrow)

　　_____

4. (you / sleep / will / well tonight)

　　_____

B. Use the verbs in parentheses to make correct questions with **be going to**.

Example: _____Are_____ you (study) ___going to study___ for the test?

1. _____ your mother (bake) _____ some cookies for us?

2. _____ I (be) _____ at the party tomorrow? Sure!

3. _____ it (rain) _____ today?

4. _____ we (practice) _____ soccer on Saturday?

Name _____ Date _____

● Grammar Expansion
Future Perfect Tense

Future Perfect Tense			
subject	**will have**	**past participle**	
I / She / He / It We / You / They	**will have**	finished	our homework by 9:00.

Use the future perfect tense to talk about something that will happen before a later time in the future.

A. Complete the sentences with the future perfect tense of the verbs.

Example: I cannot watch television until my homework is finished. That is

OK because I (finish) _____will have finished_____ my homework before my

favorite program starts.

1. Alma walks five miles each day. By the end of the year,

   she (walk) _____ 1,800 miles!

2. Oscar and Inez love museums. Soon they (visit) _____

   all of the museums in our city.

3. My dad (work) _____ at the same job for ten years at the

   end of this year.

4. My grandfather and I are planting seeds. When we finish,

   we (plant) _____ over one thousand seeds.

B. Complete these sentences about yourself. Use the future perfect tense.

Example: _____Before this week is over, I will have completed my science project_____.

1. Before this school year is over, I _____.

2. When I finish high school, I _____.

3. By the time I am 20, I _____.

Name _____ Date _____

● **Writing Assignment**   *Use with student book pages 220–221.*
  Personal Narrative: Write a Diary Entry

Use this chart to help you prewrite your diary entry.

1. List the people involved in the conflict.

   _____   _____

   _____   _____

2. Describe the conflict. Include your thoughts and experiences so far.

   _____

   _____

   _____

   _____

   _____

3. Describe how you might use the conflict resolution ideas from the reading.
   a. Describe the trigger. Figure out what is upsetting you.

   _____

   _____

   _____

   b. Describe what you have to gain by resolving the conflict.

   _____

   _____

   _____

   c. Try to put yourself in the other person's place. What is he or she feeling?

   _____

   _____

   _____

Name _____   Date _____

● **Writing Assignment**   *Use with student book page 221.*
Writing Support

> **Grammar: Adverbs of Frequency**
> Adverbs of frequency tell how often something happens. They include:
>
> never   rarely   sometimes   often   usually   always
> ◄───►
> 0% of the time   100% of the time

A.   Choose the correct adverb of frequency.

Example: I almost never eat tomatoes.

I ((rarely) / always) eat tomatoes.

1. Alan goes to bed by midnight 100% of the time.

   Alan (usually / always) goes to bed by midnight.

2. I watch television almost every night.

   I (rarely / usually) watch television at night.

3. It rains only ten days a year in the desert.

   It (often / rarely) rains in the desert.

4. The bus does not stop at this corner.

   The bus (sometimes / never) stops at this corner.

5. I have soup for lunch once or twice a month.

   I (sometimes / never) have soup for lunch.

B.   Complete the sentences with an adverb of frequency. Tell the truth.

Example: I _____ *often* _____ go to the movies.

1. I _____ eat vegetables.

2. My friends _____ come to my house.

3. I _____ do my homework.

4. I _____ get good grades on tests.

166

Name _____ Date _____

● Writing Assignment

Use with student book page 221.

Revising Activity

Read the diary entry.

April 11, 2005

(1) What a day! (2) I had an argument with my best friend. (3) He and I were walking home from school and I told him I wanted to borrow his bike. (4) He said it was brand-new and he did not want to lend it to anyone. (5) I reminded him that I let him take my laptop home last weekend. (6) It really bothers me when I am generous and other people are not. (7) So, anyway, I walked away without saying good-bye. (8) Maybe I should call him and try to work things out. (9) I know we would both feel a lot happier if I did that.

—Roberto

A. Write one or more sentence numbers to show where each item below appears in the diary entry. Two items do not appear in the diary entry at all. Mark them with an "X." Some appear more than once.

Example: _____3, 4, 5_____ a description of a conflict

1. _____ the name of the other person involved in the conflict

2. _____ a description of what triggers the person's anger

3. _____ a description of what the person can gain by resolving the conflict

4. _____ words that show someone understanding another person's place

5. _____ an example of cause and effect

B. Which of the five items listed in Exercise A are missing from the diary entry? For each missing item, rewrite a sentence or add a sentence to the passage.

Example:

Missing item: ____the name of the other person involved in the conflict____

Sentence: ____Karim and I were walking home from school and I told him . . .____

Missing item: _____

Sentence: _____

Name _____   Date _____

● Writing Assignment
Editing Activity

Use with student book page 221.

A. Read this diary entry and decide how to make it better. Use the editing marks on page 419 of your student book to mark changes. Pay attention to these items:

> 1. Put the date at the top right corner of the diary entry.
> 2. Sign your name.
> 3. Capitalize the first word of each sentence.
> 4. Use **will** and **be going to** in the diary entry.

Today I had a disagreement with the librarian. She said I did not return the Harry Potter book I borrowed. but I know I returned it. I remember dropping it off at the library on the way to class last Friday. Anyway, she said I cannot take any more books. I have a term paper assignment. I write it next weekend. that means I need to take some books from the library tomorrow. What should I do? I know! I ask my sister to talk with the librarian. my sister is a library aid. I am sure that helps.

—Nina Blanco

B. Now rewrite the diary entry. Make the changes you marked above.

_____

_____

_____

_____

_____

_____

_____

_____

_____

Name _____ Date _____

Vocabulary From the Reading

Use with student book page 226.

> **Key Vocabulary**
>
> crop   product
> factory *(singular)* /   region
> factories *(plural)*   technology
> manufacture

A. Write the Key Vocabulary word for each definition.

Word	Definition
Example: _manufacture_	make a product by hand or with machines
1. _____	something that is made or produced in a factory
2. _____	plants grown by a farmer
3. _____	a geographical area
4. _____	scientific ideas and equipment
5. _____	a place where things are made using machines

B. Complete each sentence with a Key Vocabulary word.

Example: The most valuable _____ _crop_ _____ they grow on this farm is corn.

1. It never snows in this _____.

2. The _____ that computers use is very complex.

3. They do not _____ cars in Alaska.

4. The parts of most cars come from many different _____.

5. You can buy computers and other electronic _____ in this store.

C. Use the Key Vocabulary words to describe things about your life.

Example: _There are a lot of lakes in my region of California._

1. _____

2. _____

3. _____

Name _____   Date _____

● Reading Strategy
Use with student book page 227.

Put Text Information in an Outline

Putting information in an **outline** with **numerals** can clarify your understanding.

Academic Vocabulary for the Reading Strategy	
Word	Explanation
outline	a summary of the main ideas of something
numeral	a symbol that represents (stands for) a number

Read the two paragraphs. Then complete the outline.

The Civil War had both positive and negative results. Two very good things came out of this conflict. Perhaps the most important was the end of slavery. On September 22, 1862, President Lincoln issued the Emancipation Proclamation. This proclamation stated that all former slaves were now free. There was a second result of the war. Before the war, people felt like they were citizens of a state. After the war, people began to feel like citizens of the United States.

However, there were also some very negative results from the war. Many homes and businesses in the South were destroyed, and at least 600,000 men were killed. Also, many white southerners blamed the former slaves for all the death and destruction.

Put the information that you remember from the reading in outline form.

I. ___Positive Results of Civil War_____

     A. _____

     B. _____

II. _____

     A. _____

     B. _____

     C. _____

Name _____ Date _____

● Text Genre

Use with student book page 228.

Informational Text: Textbook

Informational Text	
headings	titles of major sections
subheadings	titles that divide major sections into smaller sections
graphics	visual features, such as pictures, maps, graphs, and charts
captions	words that explain graphics

Read the passage. Then complete the chart below.

Settling the American West

Early Expansion

Soon after the United States won its independence in 1776, thousands of individuals and families began to move westward. In 1803, the U.S. purchased a large area of the continent from France. It gave western farmers access to shipping in the Mississippi River.

Settlers come to the western frontier.

Removal of Native Americans

As more settlers began to move west, the government began to gather Native Americans in special areas called **reservations.** This resulted in many of these original peoples losing the land that had been theirs for thousands of years.

Features of the Text	Examples from the Text
Example: heading	Settling the American West
1. subheadings	
2. graphic	
3. caption	

Name _____ Date _____

● **Reading Comprehension** *Use with student book page 235.*

Academic Vocabulary for the Reading Comprehension Questions	
Word	**Explanation**
summarize	to give a brief statement of the most important features of something
text	written material

A. **Outline the passage.** Look at the text on page 171 of this book. Then use the form below to outline the information in it.

Settling the American West

I. _____

    A. _____

    B. _____

II. _____

    A. _____

    B. _____

B. **Write your response.** Summarize the main causes of the Civil War. Do you think the Civil War was necessary? How could the conflict have been solved in different ways?

_____

_____

_____

C. **Assess the reading strategy.** Now you have practiced putting text information in outline form. How does it help you understand the text and remember the information?

_____

_____

_____

Name _____ Date _____

● Text Element

Graphs

Use with student book page 235.

Some Types of Graphs	
Graph Type	**Explanation**
pie charts	Pie charts show the size relationship of many parts to a whole.
bar graphs	Bar graphs show changes over time.
line graphs	Line graphs also show changes over time.

A. Label the graphs below. Use the words **line graph, pie chart,** and **bar graph.**

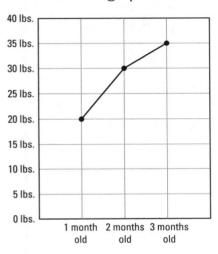

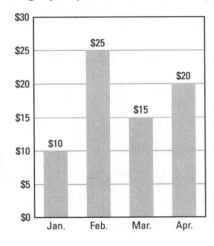

1. _____   2. _____

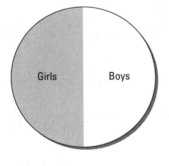

3. _____

B. Complete the sentences. Use the words **pie charts, bar graphs,** and **line graphs.**

1. _____ show the size relationship of one thing to another.

2. _____ and _____ show changes over time.

173

Name _____ Date _____

● Vocabulary From the Reading

Use with student book page 236.

> **Key Vocabulary**
>
> bragging   proud
> heal   shrink

A. Write the Key Vocabulary word for each definition.

Word	Definition
Example: _____*heal*_____	cure; make someone healthy again
1. _____	boasting; talking proudly about yourself
2. _____	having a very good opinion of yourself
3. _____	become smaller

B. Complete each sentence. Use a Key Vocabulary word in your answer.

Example: Why are you washing your socks in cold water?

        I do not want them to _____*shrink*_____.

1. How do you feel about your grades?

    I am _____ of all the As I have on my report card.

2. Is Barry telling the truth about how big a fish he caught?

    Yes, he is. He is _____.

3. Can I wash this sweater in hot water?

    No, it will _____, and it will be too small for you.

4. Why are you going to the doctor?

    I want her to _____ this rash on my hands.

C. Answer the questions. Use as many of the Key Vocabulary words as you can.

1 Why do people use a bandage on a cut?

_____

2. Do most people dislike their nationality?

_____

3. Do ice cubes get bigger in hot water?

_____

Name _____ Date _____

● Reading Strategy
Identify Cause and Effect

Use with student book page 237.

> Sometimes one event makes another one happen. This is called **cause** and **effect**.

A. Look at Chart #1. You are given a single cause. List two possible effects.

Chart #1. Cause		Effect
Your uncle wins the lottery. ⟶		**Example:** _He moves to California._ 1. _____ _____ 2. _____ _____

Look at Chart #2. You are given a single effect. List three possible causes.

Chart #2. Cause		Effect
1. _____ _____ 2. _____ _____ 3. _____ _____	⟶	Our soccer team lost Friday night.

B. Now list some cause-and-effect relationships from your life in Chart #3.

Chart #3. Cause		Effect
1. _____ _____ 2. _____ _____ 3. _____ _____	⟶	1. _____ _____ 2. _____ _____ 3. _____ _____

Name _____ Date _____

● Text Genre
Fable

Use with student book page 237.

Fable	
lesson or moral	fables usually teach something or show how to behave
simplicity	the stories are simple; the conflicts are clear
animal or object characters	the characters are often not human
personification	the non-human characters often have human qualities such as goodness

Read this fable.

The Sad Story of the Lion

Once there was a dangerous lion. He often ate smaller animals. After many years, the rabbit went to the other animals and said, "We have a problem with the lion. We must end it. I have an idea." The other animals listened to the rabbit's plan, and they agreed that it might work.

The next day, the rabbit went to the lion. When the lion saw the rabbit, he said, "Why are you here? I think I will eat you." The rabbit said, "Oh, do not eat me! I came to tell you about the new lion." "A new lion in my jungle?" roared the lion. "Take me to him!"

The rabbit led the lion to a deep well. The lion saw his reflection in the water and roared. The echo bounced back at him. "I am the only king of this jungle!" he roared. The same words echoed back. The lion was so angry he jumped into the well toward the other lion and no one ever saw him again.

Choose the best answer for each question.

Example: __C__ The lion is the personification of

    a. health

    b. kindness

    c. evil

1. ___ The rabbit is the personification of

    a. intelligence

    b. silliness

    c. generosity

2. ___ The story is a conflict between

    a. rich and poor

    b. good and evil

    c. old and young

3. ___ This fable is a ___ story.

    a. true

    b. happy

    c. simple

4. The moral of the story is ___

    a. to move quickly to save yourself.

    b. that good can triumph over evil.

    c. that lions are not very intelligent.

● Reading Comprehension

Use with student book page 241.

A. **Retell the fable.** Include at least two examples of cause and effect you discovered in the text.

_____

_____

_____

_____

_____

_____

_____

B. **Write your response.** Summarize your feelings about fables like this one. Do you enjoy them? Do you think they teach us anything? Why or why not?

_____

_____

_____

_____

_____

C. **Assess the reading strategy.** As you read "The Quarrel Between Wind and Thunder," you were asked to look for examples of cause and effect. How did studying these examples help you understand the story?

_____

_____

_____

_____

_____

Name _____   Date _____

● Spelling

Use with student book page 241.

Abbreviations of State Names

Alabama	AL	Hawaii	HI	Massachusetts	MA	New Mexico	NM	South Dakota	SD
Alaska	AK	Idaho	ID	Michigan	MI	New York	NY	Tennessee	TN
Arizona	AZ	Illinois	IL	Minnesota	MN	North Carolina	NC	Texas	TX
Arkansas	AR	Indiana	IN	Mississippi	MS	North Dakota	ND	Utah	UT
California	CA	Iowa	IA	Missouri	MO	Ohio	OH	Vermont	VT
Colorado	CO	Kansas	KS	Montana	MT	Oklahoma	OK	Virginia	VA
Connecticut	CT	Kentucky	KY	Nebraska	NE	Oregon	OR	Washington	WA
Delaware	DE	Louisiana	LA	Nevada	NV	Pennsylvania	PA	West Virginia	WV
Florida	LF	Maine	ME	New Hampshire	NH	Rhode Island	RI	Wisconsin	WI
Georgia	GA	Maryland	MD	New Jersey	NJ	South Carolina	SC	Wyoming	WY
								District of Columbia	DC

A. Match each underlined state name with the correct abbreviation.

Example: __c__ Plantation owners grew cotton in <u>Mississippi</u>.   a. MI

1. _____ <u>Massachusetts</u> had many textile mills.   b. NC

2. _____ There were large factories in <u>New York</u>.   ~~c. MS~~

3. _____ <u>North Carolina</u> was a Confederate state.   d. ME

4. _____ A lot of wheat is grown in <u>Nebraska</u>.   e. MA

5. _____ Cars are manufactured in <u>Michigan</u>.   f. NE

6. _____ Fishing is a big industry in <u>Maine</u>.   g. NY

B. Write the address of your school using the correct state name abbreviation.

_____

Name _____ Date _____

● Writing Conventions

Use with student book page 241.

Capitalization: Using Capital Letters

Capital letters are used to start sentences and for many other purposes.

1. For a title used as a name: Have you seen **G**randmother?

2. For abbreviations of titles: **Ms**. Costas teaches math.

3. For regions of a county: It is cold in the **N**orth.

4. With historical events and documents: **C**ivil **W**ar, the **C**onstitution

5. With the names of academic courses: **A**lgebra I, **A**dvanced **B**iology

6. With proper nouns: **P**aul **S**mith, **P**ablo's **C**afé

A. Rewrite the following sentences. Be sure to use capital letters correctly.

Example: john hancock signed the declaration of independence.

John Hancock singed the Declaration of Independence.

1. the rocky mountains are tall. _____

2. did grandfather have a chevrolet? _____

3. does mr. orlando teach geography I? _____

4. is mother at smith's hardware store? _____

5. reed college is in portland, oregon. _____

6. was mark hamill in *star wars*? _____

B. Answer the questions with true information. Write complete sentences.

Example: Which region of the United States do you live in?

I live in the Southwest.

1. What is the name of your best friend?

_____

2. What historical events are interesting to you?

_____

3. What is your favorite restaurant?

_____

Name _____ Date _____

● Vocabulary Development

Prefixes: un-, dis-

Use with student book page 243.

Word	Prefix	Root Word	Word in Context
unfair	**un-**	fair	Some people thought that slavery was wrong and **un**fair.
disagreement	**dis-**	agreement	The **dis**agreement over slavery led to arguments.

A. Match each word with the correct definition

Example: __b__ dishonest

1. _____ unhappy

2. _____ unfair

3. _____ dislike

4. _____ unhealthy

5. _____ disagree

a. hate

b. not telling the truth

c. have a different opinion

d. sad

e. not good for you

f. not reasonable

B. Complete each sentence with the prefix **dis-** or **un-** + a word from the box.

~~agree~~	like	honest	fair	happy	healthy

Example: I sometimes __disagree__ with my friends.

1. Eating too much is _____.

2. I _____ going to bed early.

3. Sam was _____ because he could not go out with us.

4. It is _____ to copy someone else's homework.

5. It is _____ for one team to have more members than the other.

Name _____ Date _____

● Grammar

Some, Any

Use with student book pages 244–245.

Some, Any		
	When to Use	**Example**
some	Use **some** in affirmative statements.	The North and South disagreed about **some** important issues.
any	Use **any** in negative statements.	The North didn't want **any** slavery.
	Use **any** in questions.	Was there **any** slavery in the North?

A. Circle the correct answer.

Example: Do you have (some / (any)) brothers or sisters?

1. I do not want (some / any) coffee, thanks.

2. Are there (some / any) cookies in the jar?

3. There are (some / any) apples in the refrigerator.

4. Lisa made (some / any) muffins last night.

5. I did not buy (some / any) CDs last month.

B. Complete the sentences. Use **some** or **any**.

Example: Jack has some money. Did he give you _____*any*_____?

1. I have _____ paper clips. Do you need one?

2. I need _____ new clothes.

3. I do not have _____ notebook paper.

4. There are _____ blue pens in the drawer.

5. There is not _____ peanut butter in the cabinet.

Name _____ Date _____

● Grammar Expansion
Indefinite Pronouns

Someone, somewhere, something, anyone, anywhere, and **anything** are called indefinite pronouns. We use these words to talk about people, places, and things, but we do not give exact information about them.

Indefinite Pronouns		
	When to Use	**Examples**
someone somewhere something	Use in affirmative statements.	I saw **someone** in the library. We went **somewhere** last night. I learned **something** interesting.
anyone anywhere anything	Use in questions and in negative statements.	Did you go **anywhere** after class? I do not know **anyone** from Cuba. Didn't you eat **anything** yesterday?

A. Choose the correct answers.

Example: __*a*__ Did you find _____ under the sofa?
      a. anything   b. anywhere

1. _____ I know _____ from Iran.
    a. anyone   b. someone

2. _____ Let me tell you _____.
    a. anything b. something

3. _____ I do not talk to _____ in class.
    a. someone b. anyone

4. _____ Let's go _____ after class!
    a. anywhere b. somewhere

5. _____ I did not go _____ on Sunday.
    a. anywhere b. somewhere

6. _____ Do you want me to buy _____?
    a. anything b. anywhere

B. Complete the sentences with the correct indefinite pronoun. You can choose from the chart at the top of the page.

Example: Do you go _____*anywhere*_____ on Saturday nights?

1. I bought you _____ at the jewelry store.

2. _____ asked me what your name is.

3. You should never put _____ in your ears.

4. I do not let _____ read my diary.

● Grammar Expansion

A lot of and *Many* in Affirmative Sentences

A **count noun** is something we can count: one apple, two apples, three apples.

A **noncount noun** cannot be counted: water, bread, happiness.

	a lot of / many	plural count noun
The South had	a lot of	plantations.
The North had	many	factories.

	a lot of	noncount noun
The South has	a lot of	sunshine.
The North has		snow.

Rewrite the sentences changing **a lot of** to **many** if possible. If you cannot use **many,** leave the sentence alone.

Example: There are a lot of books on the shelf.

There are many books on the shelf. _____

1. I have a lot of time before class.

   _____

2. There are a lot of windows in this room.

   _____

3. I have a lot of homework this weekend.

   _____

4. We have a lot of books to read this semester.

   _____

5. I eat a lot of bread every day.

   _____

6. Glen has visited a lot of countries.

   _____

Name _____ Date _____

● Grammar Expansion

A lot of, *Much*, and *Many* in Negative Sentences

	a lot of / many	Plural Count Nouns
I do not have	**a lot of**	CDs.
The house does not have	**many**	rooms.

	a lot of / much	Noncount Nouns
She does not have	**a lot of**	money.
The desert does not get	**much**	rain.

A. Complete each sentence with the correct word or phrase in parentheses.

Example: Our town does not have _____*a lot of*_____ crime. (many / a lot of)

1. She has _____ homework. (many / a lot of)

2. He does not have _____ money. (much / many)

3. I did not get _____ phone calls today. (a lot of / much)

4. There are not _____ apples in the refrigerator. (many / much)

5. She did not give me _____ soup. (many / much)

6. There is not _____ sugar in the bowl. (many / much)

B. Write five sentences that tell what is in your refrigerator at home. Use each of the following words: **some, any, many, much,** and **a lot of,** at least once in your sentences.

Example: _In my refrigerator, there is some bread, but there are not many eggs._

1. _____

2. _____

3. _____

4. _____

5. _____

Name _____ Date _____

● Writing Assignment
Use with student book pages 246–247.

Persuasive Writing: Write a Newspaper Editorial

Use this chart to help you plan your newspaper editorial.

1. Choose a topic that has two sides: _____

2. Choose a side to take: _____
_____

3. Find information about the topic. You can use the Internet, an encyclopedia, or library books to gather more information. Take notes in the space below.

Source # 1: _____

Notes: _____
_____
_____

Source # 2: _____

Notes: _____
_____
_____

Source # 3: _____

Notes: _____
_____
_____

4. Think of a title for your editorial: _____
_____

5. Include a statement of your opinion in the first paragraph:
_____
_____

6. Restate your opinion in different words in the conclusion:
_____
_____

Name _____ Date _____

● **Writing Assignment**
Writing Support

Use with student book page 247.

Grammar: Definite Article: *the*

Use **the** before geographical areas, names of rivers, and points on the globe.

Do **not** use **the** before names of continents, countries*, cities, states, streets, lakes, and mountains.

*Exceptions include **the** United States, *the* United Kingdom, and *the* Netherlands.

A. Write **the** when it is needed. Write **X** when it is not needed.

Example: ___The___ South Pole is in ___X___ Antarctica.

1. _____ Mississippi River ends in _____ New Orleans.

2. _____ Salt Lake City is near _____ Salt Lake.

3. _____ Egypt is in _____ Middle East.

4. _____ Hudson River flows through _____ New York City and

_____ New Jersey.

B. Correct these sentences. Cross out or add the word **the** where necessary. Use the carat symbol (∧), where you want to insert **the.**

Example: I live on ~~the~~ State Street.

1. The Mount McKinley is in Alaska.

2. The Los Angeles is the biggest city in United States.

3. Equator runs through the Ecuador.

4. Some small states like the Rhode Island are found in North.

C. Write about streets, cities, mountains, rivers, etc., in your country. Be sure to use the definite article **the** correctly.

Example: _Okinawa is in the Pacific Ocean._ _____

1. _____

2. _____

3. _____

● Writing Assignment

Revising Activity

Use with student book page 247.

Read over your newspaper editorial carefully. Answer the following questions. You may wish to use the answers to revise your letter.

1. Is your title strong? Does it make people want to read your letter? You might try writing down some other ideas for a title.

   _____

2. Does your editorial contain helpful information? Which points are stronger? Which ones are weaker? Try finding more information on the Internet, in an encyclopedia, or in a book. Look in two additional sources.

   New Source #1: _____

   Notes: _____

   _____

   New Source #2: _____

   Notes: _____

   _____

3. Study each paragraph carefully.

   First paragraph: Is your statement of opinion clear and complete? Try rewriting it here with stronger and clearer words.

   _____

   _____

   Middle paragraphs: Do these paragraphs strongly support your main idea? Try to remove the weaker sentences and to write stronger ones here.

   _____

   _____

   Final paragraph: Does this paragraph restate the opinion from the first paragraph? Try rewriting your opinion again here clearly.

   _____

   _____

Name _____ Date _____

● Writing Assignment

Use with student book page 247.

Editing Activity

A. Read this newspaper editorial and decide how to make it better. Use the editing marks on page 419 of your student book to mark changes. Pay attention to these items:

1. Be sure to use capital letters correctly.
2. Use words with the prefixes **un-** and **dis-** correctly.
3. Use the indefinite pronouns **someone, somewhere, something, anyone, anywhere,** and **anything** correctly.
4. Use the definite article **the** correctly.

Here is anything that really bothers me! I hate buying somewhere at a store and when I get it home, it is no good. yesterday I bought a quart of milk at the deli on the corner of the Center Street and the River Road. I paid two dollars. When I got home, I found the milk was spoiled. I called the store to complain and anyone told me to call the milk company. so I called the milk company and someone said they would send me a refund. Right! They are totally independable!

B. Now rewrite the newspaper editorial. Make the changes you marked above.

_____

_____

_____

_____

_____

_____

_____

_____

_____

Name _____ Date _____

● Vocabulary From the Reading

Use with student book page 264.

> **Key Vocabulary**
> damage   injury *(singular)* /
> force   injuries *(plural)*
> freezing   rescue
>   supplies

A. Write the Key Vocabulary word for each definition.

Word	Definition
Example: _damage_	hurt; injure
1. _____	materials needed to do something
2. _____	use power to make someone do something
3. _____	save from a dangerous situation
4. _____	extremely cold
5. _____	a wound; something that damages a part of the body

B. Rewrite each sentence. Replace the underlined word or words with a Key Vocabulary word.

Example: They tried to <u>save</u> the drowning animal.

     They tried to rescue the drowning animal.

1. Fortunately, the man did not have a serious <u>wound</u>.

_____

2. There was a <u>very cold</u> wind last night.

_____

3. The storm did not <u>harm</u> the house.

_____

4. They tried to <u>require</u> everyone to wear a uniform.

_____

5. We picked up the <u>materials we needed</u> at the store.

_____

Name _____ Date _____

● **Reading Strategy**   *Use with student book page 265.*
Recognize Chronological Order

> The order in which events happen in a story is called **chronological order.** Writers often **indicate** chronological order with words like **first, next,** and **finally.**

Academic Vocabulary for the Reading Strategy		
Word	**Explanation**	
chronological	arranged in the order in which events happen over time	
indicate	to show where or what something is	

A.   Read the following sentences. Circle the time words in each sentence.

Example: (Then) I got on the bus.

1.   Next, I purchased a sandwich and some fruit.

2.   Finally, I remembered where it was.

3.   Before I got on the bus yesterday, I bought a newspaper.

4.   After about an hour, I got hungry.

5.   Then I asked the person next to me if she had seen it.

B.   Reread the sentences in Exercise A. Then use them to write a paragraph in the correct chronological order. Include these two extra sentences:

It was sitting on the ground next to the newspaper stand.

I looked in my backpack, but the food was not there.

Before I got on the bus yesterday, I bought a newspaper.

_____

_____

_____

_____

_____

_____

Name _____   Date _____

● Text Genre
Graphic Novel

Use with student book page 266.

Graphic Novel	
story	can be either fiction (made up) or nonfiction (true)
varied story genres	can be historical fiction, action-adventure, fantasy, or science fiction
illustrations	comic book style illustrations are on every page
dialogue	conversation between characters; the dialogue often appears in "speech bubbles"

A.   Write **T** for **true** and **F** for **false**.

Example: __T__ *The Adventures of Superman* is an action-adventure.

1. _____ A story about a war can be historical fiction.

2. _____ A chapter in a history book can contain fiction.

3. _____ Stories of people living on Mars are science fiction or fantasy.

4. _____ Nonfiction stories must contain only true facts.

5. _____ A story about hunting animals in the jungle is an action-adventure story.

B.   Think of a scene where two people are talking to each other. You can use a scene from a book, television, a movie, or your own life. Draw an illustration of the two people. Write their dialogue in the speech bubbles.

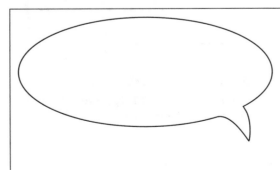
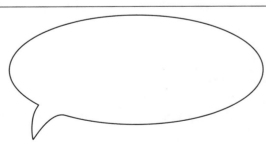

Name _____   Date _____

● Reading Comprehension

Use with student book page 277.

Academic Vocabulary for the Reading Comprehension Questions	
Word	Explanation
contribute	to give; to participate positively in something
aid	to assist or help

A.   Retell the story. Tell the main events of the story. Use the words **before, after, first, next, then,** and **finally** to make the chronological order clear.

_____

_____

_____

_____

_____

B.   Write your response. What did Shackelton's actions indicate about his personality? What kind of person was he? What did he contribute to the survival of the crew?

_____

_____

_____

_____

C.   Assess the reading strategy. Think back on the story about Shackelton's Antarctic expedition. What did the writer do to indicate the chronological order of the events? How did this aid your understanding of the text?

_____

_____

_____

_____

Milestones A • Copyright © Heinle

Name _____ Date _____

● Literary Element

Use with student book page 277.

Setting

> The **setting** of a story is the place and time in which the story happens. The setting often affects both the characters and the plot.

A. Read this description of a setting. Then answer the questions.

The story takes place on a tiny island near the coast of Maine. Three children, ages 10, 14, and 16, live there with their parents. No one else lives on the island, and the family goes to the mainland only once a month.

Example: How might the setting affect the parents?

It might be hard to find a job on the island.

1. How might the setting affect the children?

_____

2. Describe the plot of a story that could happen there.

_____

_____

_____

B. Read this description of the characters and the plot in a story. Tell what kind of setting would be good for this story. Give reasons for your answer.

Three teenage boys decide to get jobs so they can make some money. First, they try cleaning people's apartments. They do not like that, so they try delivering boxes for a big store. Finally, they start a dog-walking business that they really enjoy.

_____

_____

_____

_____

_____

Name _____ Date _____

● Vocabulary From the Reading

Use with student book page 278.

> **Key Vocabulary**
>
> attitude   skill
> equipment   task
> knowledge

A. Write the Key Vocabulary word for each definition.

Word	Definition
Example: _____skill_____	ability to do something well
1._____	items needed for a useful purpose
2._____	assignment, job to be performed
3._____	a feeling about or toward someone or something
4._____	information about something

B. Circle the correct word in each sentence.

Example: My dentist bought some new (attitude /(equipment)) for his office.

1. Public libraries contain a great deal of (attitude / knowledge).

2. Cleaning my room is not my favorite (task / knowledge).

3. He has a good (task / attitude) about his schoolwork.

4. The ability to memorize words is a useful (skill / attitude).

5. Running is a sport that does not require any (task / equipment).

C. Complete the answers. Use a Key Vocabulary word in each answer.

Example: What job do you enjoy doing around the house?

My favorite _____task_____ is ironing.

1. Why read books? They contain so much _____.

2. Drawing pictures of people is a _____ that I never learned.

3. How do you feel about getting up early? I have a bad _____ about it.

Milestones A • Copyright © Heinle

Name _____ Date _____

● Reading Strategy
Think Aloud

Use with student book page 279.

When you **think aloud** about something, you can find the answer more easily.

Read each problem below. Then write what you might say aloud as you solve the problem.

Example: You want a cell phone, but your parents will not buy one for you.

First, I should figure out why they will not buy me a cell phone. Maybe it's because they do not want to pay for it. I could promise not to make too many calls. Or I could get a part-time job and pay for it myself.

1. You and your sister bought a CD player to share for $60. You paid the entire cost. Your mother has offered to pay for half. How much should she give you? How much should your sister give you?

_____

_____

_____

2. You have about 12 hours of work left on a school project. It is Friday and the paper is due on Monday morning. You want to divide up the work so it does not feel so difficult. How much work should you do each day?

_____

_____

_____

3. Your brother will not let you use the computer for homework because he is playing video games.

_____

_____

_____

Name _____   Date _____

● Text Genre

Use with student book page 279.

Informational Text

> An **informational text** includes facts and information. It may also include questions and problems.

Read this informational text.

1 Earth's climate is changing all the time. Until 14,000 years ago, much of North America was covered with ice. By 7,000 years ago, most of that ice was gone. At other times in the past, floods covered parts of the earth. Why do you think Earth's climate has changed so much over the years?

2 The average temperature on Earth also goes up and down. It usually takes thousands of years for the temperature to change by one degree Celsius. However, recently the temperature has been rising much faster. This is called **global warming.** Some scientists believe that this change is the result of human activity. Think for a moment about what you may be doing to speed up global warming.

Answer these questions about the informational text.

Example: What is one fact the writer gives us?

Much of North America was covered with ice 14,000 years ago.

1. What are some other facts the writer includes?

   _____

   _____

   _____

2. What information does the writer give about global warming?

   _____

   _____

   _____

3. Write down the question the writer asks the reader.

   _____

4. Write down the problem the writer asks the reader to think about.

   _____

Milestones A • Copyright © Heinle

Name _____ Date _____

● Reading Comprehension

Use with student book page 283.

A. Recall the problems. What were the problems faced by the people who were lost in the forest in *Using Math to Survive in the Wild*? Use the think-aloud technique to show what each person can do to help the group survive.

_____

_____

_____

_____

_____

_____

B. Write your response. How do you think you would react to being lost in the woods? What do you think you would contribute to the effort to survive?

_____

_____

_____

_____

_____

C. Assess the reading strategy. Think about what you learned from *Using Math to Survive in the Wild*. How did the think aloud technique help you get more out of the story?

_____

_____

_____

_____

_____

Name _____ Date _____

● Spelling
Ordinal Numbers

Use with student book page 283.

> The numbers we use to count things are called **cardinal numbers**, for example, **one, two, three**. The numbers we use to tell the position of something in a series are called **ordinal numbers**. We sometimes abbreviate the ordinal numbers with a numeral followed by the letters **st, nd**, or **th**.

Numerals	Cardinal Numbers	Ordinal Numbers	Abbreviations of Ordinal Numbers
1	one	first	1st
2	two	second	2nd
3	three	third	3rd
4	four	fourth	4th
5	five	fifth	5th
6	six	sixth	6th
7	seven	seventh	7th
8	eight	eighth	8th
9	nine	ninth	9th
10	ten	tenth	10th

A. Complete the sentences with the correct ordinal number or cardinal number. Use the numerals in parentheses.

Example: That is your ____third____ glass of milk this morning! (3)

1. We live on the _____ floor of the building. (5)

2. Can I borrow _____ dollars? (2)

3. He was the _____ person in line. (9)

B. Write the abbreviations for the underlined ordinal numbers.

Example: ____2nd____ the second floor

1. _____ my fourth apple

2. _____ on Fifth Street

3. _____ the tenth time

4. _____ in the seventh grade

5. _____ the first time I met him

6. _____ the eighth day in a row

Name _____ Date _____

● Writing Conventions

Use with student book page 283.

Capitalization: Place Names

> Use capital letters for the first letters of place names. Capitalize the names of continents, countries, regions, states, and cities.
> Fresnillo is the largest city in the state of **Zacatecas** in **Mexico**.

A. Rewrite the following sentences. Be sure to use capital letters correctly.

Example: Many explorers have visited the north pole.

Many explorers have visited the North Pole.

1. california is in the west, and its capital is sacramento.

_____

2. He traveled all over asia, visiting laos and thailand.

_____

3. montreal is the capital of the province of quebec.

_____

4. china is the largest country in the far east.

_____

5. The continent of australia is also a country.

_____

6. johannesburg is the largest city in south africa.

_____

B. Write sentences about where you live. Use a capitalized place name in each one.

Example: _I live in the continent of North America._

1. _____

2. _____

3. _____

4. _____

5. _____

199

Name _____   Date _____

● Vocabulary Development
Use with student book page 285.

The Adverb Suffix -ly

Adverb	Adjective	+ -ly
quickly	quick	-ly
safely	safe	-ly

A. Match the beginning of each sentence with its ending.

Example: __*g*__ She is a good dancer. She dances

1. _____ She was not wrong. She answered the question

2. _____ Hurry up. We need to move

3. _____ I do not take chances. I drive very

4. _____ He has a lot of accidents. He drives

5. _____ Not so fast! Speak more

6. _____ I cannot hear you. Please speak more

7. _____ He practiced the song until he could sing it

a. perfectly

b. badly

c. carefully

d. slowly

e. correctly

f. loudly

g. ~~beautifully~~

h. quickly

B. Write an original sentence using these adverbs.

Example: (quickly) _He closed the door quickly._____

1. (softly) _____

2. (nicely) _____

3. (truthfully) _____

4. (safely) _____

5. (quickly) _____

6. (perfectly) _____

Name _____ Date _____

● Grammar

Use with student book page 286.

The Present Progressive Tense: Spelling and Review

Spelling of Verbs Ending in *-ing*		
Base Form	**Spelling in the Present Progressive**	**Rule**
work	work**ing**	For most verbs: add **-ing**.
write dance	writ**ing** danc**ing**	For verbs that end in a **consonant + e:** drop the **e** and add **-ing**.
sit plan	sit**ting** plan**ning**	For one-syllable verbs ending in **one vowel + one consonant:** double the consonant and add **-ing**.
play read listen think	play**ing** read**ing** listen**ing** think**ing**	Do not double the last consonant before **-ing** when the verb: • ends in **w, x,** or **y;** • ends in two vowels and then one consonant; • has more than one syllable (when the stress is on the first syllable) • ends in two or more consonants.

A. Write the simple form and the **-ing** form of the verbs in the box in the correct place on the chart.

fix   look   get   drop   row   read   feel   mix   hit   fly   tap   fail

1. One-syllable verbs that end in one vowel + one consonant.	2. One-syllable verbs that end in **w, x,** or **y.**	3. One-syllable verbs that end in two vowels and then one consonant.
___ ___	*fix* *fixing*	___ ___
___ ___	___ ___	___ ___
___ ___	___ ___	___ ___
___ ___	___ ___	___ ___

Name _____ Date _____

B. Complete the sentences with the present progressive form of a verb in the box.

~~fix~~	look	plan	read	fly	fail	think

Example: The washing machine is broken, and Jim _____*is fixing*_____ it.

1. She _____ to Paris right now.

2. The students _____ a party for next Saturday night.

3. The sunset is beautiful. I _____ at it.

4. I did not study, and now I _____ math.

5. Our TV is very old, so we _____ about buying a new one.

6. He bought a book in Mexico, and now he _____ it.

C. Imagine that the teacher has given the class a ten-minute break. You can do anything you want to as long as you do not leave the room. Use the present progressive tense to describe what different students in your class are doing. Use your imagination.

Example: _I am talking with my friend, Arnold. Lidia is looking at a magazine._

_____

_____

_____

_____

_____

_____

_____

Name _____ Date _____

● Grammar

Use with student book page 287.

The Past Progressive Tense

The Past Progressive Tense		
Subject	***was / were*** **(past of *be*)**	**base verb + -*ing***
I	was	
He / She / It	was	eat**ing**.
You / We / They	were	

A. Complete each sentence with the past progressive tense of the verb in parentheses.

Example: I _____ *was eating* _____ (eat) breakfast when Alice arrived.

1. She _____ (put) ice in her water.

2. He _____ (cook) dinner when I got home.

3. I _____ (look) for my wallet, but I could not find it.

4. The teacher _____ (write) on the board when the bell rang.

5. This time last week we _____ (fly) down to Florida.

B. Rewrite these sentences using the past progressive tense.

Example: Pam is studying in the library.
> *Pam was studying in the library.*

1. My friends are wearing their team T-shirts.

_____

2. The cat is watching and waiting for the mouse to come out.

_____

3. I am waiting for the bus and reading a magazine.

_____

4. You are sitting in Bob's seat.

_____

Name _____ Date _____

C. Complete these sentences with your own ideas. Use the past progressive tense.

Example: _____ I was sitting in my seat _____ when class started today.

1. _____, but I went to the beach anyway.

2. _____, and my sister was, too.

3. _____ when the teacher walked in.

4. _____ when I woke up this morning.

5. _____ when it started snowing.

6. _____ when the phone rang.

D. Complete each sentence using the past progressive tense in each blank.

1. Yesterday, my friends and I _____ were walking _____ (walk) home from

   school. We _____ (talk) about Roberto. Then we

   saw him. He _____ (stand) by the bus stop, and he

   _____ (read) a newspaper.

2. Kenji _____ (do) his homework when Linda walked

   into the room. He _____ (try) to finish his homework

   quickly. Linda _____ (carry) his running shoes.

   Maybe he would do his homework later.

3. Last night, I _____ (watch) TV after dinner. The

   weather forecaster _____ (point) to a map of

   the U.S., and she _____ (say) that a big storm

   _____ (come). All of a sudden, I realized it

   _____ (move) toward my city!

Name _____ Date _____

● **Writing Assignment**   *Use with student book pages 288–289.*

Creative Writing: Write a Survival Journal

Write ideas for your survival journal here to help you prewrite it.

1. Choose a survival situation to write about. It can be one from the student book or a different one.

   _____

2. Make notes about the setting for your survival situation. What does the place look like?

   _____

   _____

   What does it feel like?

   _____

   _____

   What do you hear when you are there?

   _____

   _____

3. What problems do you face?

   _____

   _____

   _____

4. What solutions do you come up with?

   _____

   _____

   _____

Name _____ Date _____

● Writing Assignment
Use with student book page 289.
Writing Support

> **Spelling: Commonly Confused Words: it's / its**
>
> it's = contraction of **it is**   It's important to check your compositions.
> its = possessive of **it**   The dog has a collar around **its** neck.

A. Circle the correct word in each sentence.

Example: I'm eating a peanut butter sandwich and ((it's)/ its) very good.

1. The dog has finished all of (it's / its) food.

2. (It's / Its) exactly one o'clock.

3. This book is old. (It's / Its) pages are all dirty.

4. That coat is very nice but (it's / its) not mine.

B. Complete each sentence. Use **it's** or **its.**

Example: The library should be open, but _____it's_____ closed.

1. _____ nice to see you again!

2. I did the dishes last night. _____ your turn tonight.

3. The cat is lying on _____ back.

4. The computer is in _____ own little room.

C. Write two sentences using **it's** and two sentences using **its.**

Example: ___It's time for me to go home._____

1. (it's) _____

2. (it's) _____

3. (its) _____

4. (its) _____

Milestones A • Copyright © Heinle

Name _____ Date _____

● Writing Assignment
Revising Activity

Use with student book page 289.

An interesting survival journal entry should have the following elements:

> 1. a complete description of the setting,
> 2. an explanation of the problem,
> 3. descriptions of solutions to the problem,
> 4. clear and complete sentences throughout.

Read this survival entry. It is about a city boy who has a winter job in a restaurant at a ski resort in the mountains. He is staying with his aunt about 20 miles away.

August 12, 2007

(1) It was midnight. (2) I had worked 12 hours, and I was really tired. (3) I decided to take the back roads home, but then I almost fell asleep while driving. (4) So I decided to take a quick nap. (5) Next thing I knew, it was 2:00 in the morning, and I was freezing—really freezing! (6) I tried to start the car, but I couldn't do it. (7) I looked around. (8) There was snow everywhere. (9) I jumped out and raised the hood. (10) I moved wires, but it did not. (11) I was really shivering. (12) I was ten miles from home and had only my light waiter's coat on over my shirt. (13) I wished I had a sweater or something. (14) Maybe I could walk or run home. (15) No. It was well below zero and the wind was blowing hard. (16) Then I remembered the emergency cell phone that Aunt Helen put in the glove compartment. (17) It still worked!

A. Write one or more sentence numbers to show where each item below appears in the survival journal entry. Some sentence numbers can answer more than one question.

1. ___3___ ____ ____ ____ Sentences that explain the problem

2. ____ ____ ____ ____ Sentences that suggest possible solutions

3. ____ ____ ____ ____ Sentences that describe the setting

4. ____ ____ ____ ____ Unclear or incomplete sentences

B. Choose a sentence that is not clear and complete and rewrite it.

_____

Name _____   Date _____

● Writing Assignment
Use with student book page 289.

Editing Activity

A. Read this scene from a survival journal entry and find the mistakes. Mark them using the editing marks on page 419 in your student book. The entry should:

> 1. have a date at the top,
> 2. use the past progressive tense correctly,
> 3. use **its** and **it's** correctly,
> 4. use adverbs with **-ly** correctly.

Ryan and I was rowing the canoe across the lake when a storm came up. The sky sudden got really dark. We were about a mile from shore when we saw the first lightning strike. It's flash really scared us. We decided to head for home. "We can make it in ten minutes. Its not that far," I said. But the wind blowing very hard and we was moving very slow. The lightning seemed to be getting closer and that really scared me! But then, I saw something in the distance. Alice is driving my father's motorboat and she was heading straight toward us. My sister isn't always my favorite person, but she sure was that day.

B. Make the corrections as you rewrite the journal entry.

_____

_____

_____

_____

_____

_____

_____

_____

Name _____ Date _____

● **Vocabulary From the Reading**   *Use with student book page 294.*

> **Key Vocabulary**
>
> | | |
> |---|---|
> | destroy | sink |
> | energy | spin |
> | flooding | warning |
> | protect | |

A. Write the Key Vocabulary word for each definition.

Word	Definition
Example: _____flooding_____	covering something with water
1. _____	a sign that danger or trouble is near
2. _____	power, force
3. _____	turn around in a circle
4. _____	break down or ruin something
5. _____	guard against attack, defend
6. _____	fall below the surface

B. Complete each sentence with a Key Vocabulary word.

Example: Do you have enough _____energy_____ to walk home?

1. I watched the sun _____ into the ocean.

2. The rainstorm caused _____ all across Florida.

3. A big fire can _____ a whole house in a short time.

4. I just heard a storm _____. We may have three inches of snow today.

5. What can I do to _____ my skin from sunburn?

6. I watched the merry-go-round _____ around and around.

C. Write two sentences. Use as many of the Key Vocabulary words as you can.

1. _____

2. _____

Name _____ Date _____

● Reading Strategy

Use with student book page 295.

Identify Main Idea and Details

> The **main idea** is the most important idea in a reading. It is the **focus** of the reading. The **details** give more information.

Academic Vocabulary for the Reading Strategy	
Word	**Explanation**
focus	a thing that is of great importance, an object of attention
detail	smaller part of something larger and more important

Read the passage. Then complete the charts. Use examples from the passage.

1 Rock climbing is a dangerous sport for several reasons. First of all, climbers are usually hundreds of feet from the ground. Second, they don't wear protective clothing. Rock climbers often wear only shorts and a T-shirt. Also, rain and high winds can be very dangerous to climbers.

2 There are some things rock climbers can do to make their climbs safer. First, they should choose a route that is not too difficult for them. Second, climbers should stay close to the wall. Third, climbers should plan their next step before they take it. Making a mistake when climbing five hundred feet from the ground is not a good idea.

Paragraph #1 Main Idea	_____
Details	_____
	_____
	_____

Paragraph #2 Main Idea	_____
Details	_____
	_____
	_____

Milestones A • Copyright © Heinle

Name _____ Date _____

● Text Genre

Use with student book page 296.

Informational Text: Textbook

Textbook	
headings	titles of major sections
subheadings	titles that divide the major sections into smaller sections
graphics	visual features, such as pictures, photos, maps, graphs, and charts
captions	words that explain graphics

Read the passage and study the chart.

Hurricanes

How Hurricanes Form

1 All hurricanes begin over the ocean. As warm air rises, it meets an area of cooler air. This causes a disturbance and the air begins to move in a circular fashion. The hurricane can get larger and larger.

Naming Hurricanes

2 Before 1950, hurricanes were named for the year they occurred. They had names such as 1945A, 1945B, and so on. In 1950, weather forecasters began giving them names—female names. In 1978, they began to use both male and female names.

Some Hurricane Names Used 2003–2008					
2003	**2004**	**2005**	**2006**	**2007**	**2008**
Ana	Alex	Arlene	Alberto	Andrea	Arthur
Bill	Bonnie	Bret	Beryl	Barry	Bertha

The National Weather Service gives 50% male and 50% female names.

Complete the chart.

Features of the Text	Examples from the Text
Example: graphics	chart showing hurricane names
1. heading	
2. subheadings	
3. caption	

Name _____ Date _____

● Reading Comprehension

Use with student book page 303.

Academic Vocabulary for the Reading Comprehension Questions	
Word	Explanation
persuade	to lead a person or group to believe or do something by arguing or reasoning with them
recommend	to tell others about something one likes; to advise someone to do something

A. Recall main ideas. Write the main ideas in "The Fiercest Storms on Earth."

_____

_____

_____

_____

_____

_____

_____

B. Write your response. What would you say to persuade someone to leave an area where a hurricane is expected? What would you recommend that people do if they were in the path of a hurricane or a tornado?

_____

_____

_____

_____

C. Assess the reading strategy. Were you able to tell the difference between the main ideas and the details in the story? Why is it important to be able to do this?

_____

_____

_____

_____

Name _____ Date _____

● Text Elements
Headings and Subheadings

Use with student book page 303.

> Many informational texts have **headings** and **subheadings**.
> - Headings tell you the general subject of a large section of text.
> - Subheadings tell you the specific topics of each smaller section within the text.
> - Headings and subheadings prepare you to understand what you are going to read.

Read the passage. Then fill in the missing heading and subheadings on the lines below. Use the phrases in the box.

Getting Ready	Staying Safe during a Storm
Learning about Safety	Surviving a Hurricane

_____

_____

If you live in an area where there are hurricanes, you should be prepared. Make sure you have plenty of canned food and fresh water in the house. Always keep your car's gas tank at least half full. And during hurricane season, listen to radio and television weather forecasts every day.

_____

If you have to remain in your home during a hurricane, here is what you should do. Open some windows part way and then stay away from them. There is always a danger of breaking glass. Go to the safest part of the house. This is usually an interior hallway or a bathroom. Take a battery-operated radio with you so that you will know when it is safe to come out.

_____

There are many sources of free information about hurricane safety. You can contact your local police station, or you can look up information online. Just enter the words "Hurricane Safety" in your web browser and follow the suggested links.

Name _____ Date _____

● Vocabulary From the Reading

Use with student book page 304.

> **Key Vocabulary**
> amazed   preparations
> concentrate   tool

A. Write the Key Vocabulary word for each definition.

Word	Definition	
Example: _____*tool*_____	something that helps you do a job	
1. _____	focus on something	
2. _____	extremely surprised	
3. _____	plans and arrangements	

B. Complete each sentence. Use one of the Key Vocabulary words.

Example: We were _____*amazed*_____ when the dog actually talked.

1. Ellen was busy with the _____ for the party.

2. Did you _____ on your work, or were you daydreaming?

3. What kind of _____ did you use to fix your bicycle?

C. Answer each question. Use one of the Key Vocabulary words in your answer.

Example: Q: Why don't you study in the living room?

   A: I can't _____*concentrate*_____ with all the noise.

1. **Q:** Are you all ready to go?

   A: No, I have not made any _____ yet.

2. **Q:** What will make me a better writer?

   A: Well, a dictionary is a useful _____.

3. **Q:** Peter was on time today.

   A: I know. I am _____!

4. **Q:** Should I help you?

   A: No, just _____ on your own work.

Milestones A • Copyright © Heinle

Name _____   Date _____

● **Reading Strategy**   *Use with student book page 305.*
Describe Mental Images

> Writers use **mental images** to help the reader visualize the story.

A. Read the following descriptions. Then write the words and phrases the writer uses to create a mental image.

Example: Celia's car had broken down and she was walking along a lonely, muddy road looking for help.

   lonely, muddy road
   _____

1. The room was hot and stuffy. It felt like the walls were closing in on me.

   _____

2. The baby's eyes were big and brown and wide-open. People say that little babies do not really smile, but her eyes were sparkling like sun on the water.

   _____

3. There were no other students in the library. As I walked across the floor, my footsteps exploded in the silence. The librarian looked at me through narrowed eyes.

   _____

4. This bowl of cereal is unbelievable! The chunks of bananas look like little boats and the raisins look like little islands.

   _____

B. Practice using words to create mental images.

1. Write a sentence or two about a person who needs help. Choose your words carefully to create a mental image.

   _____

   _____

2. Write a sentence or two about a situation in which you were very comfortable or very uncomfortable. Use words to create a mental image of the situation.

   _____

   _____

Name _____   Date _____

● **Text Genre**   Use with student book page 305.
  Short Story

Short Story	
characters	people in a story
setting	where a story takes place
plot	events in a story that happen in a certain order
theme	the meaning or message of the story

A.   Read the passages and answer the questions.

Passage #1

Mr. and Mrs. Milsap waited until Denny was asleep upstairs. Then they sat down at the dining room table to talk. "We can invite all his friends from school," said Mrs. Milsap. "He'll be so surprised." Mr. Milsap replied, "I know. He has no idea. This is going to be fun."

Example: In this passage, the main characters are ___c___.
  a. children
  b. teenagers
  c. adults

1. The setting is _____.
   a. a house
   b. a store
   c. a school

2. The theme is _____.
   a. traveling is fun
   b. surprising people is fun
   c. working hard brings good results

Passage #2

Bob is just finishing up his turkey sandwich. "Are you sure you don't want a bite of this?" asks Bob. "No, I'm not very hungry," answers Maria. "I'm too upset about my grade on that math test. My parents are going to be angry." Bob takes a drink of his orange juice. "I wouldn't worry too much. They know math is hard for you." "You're probably right," the girl says. "It just seems like I always have something to worry about these days."

1. The main characters are _____.
   a. boys
   b. girls
   c. a boy and a girl

2. The setting is _____.
   a. a gymnasium
   b. a school cafeteria
   c. a movie theater

3. The plot is about _____.
   a. solving problems
   b. helping other people
   c. buying something

4. The theme is _____.
   a. money causes many problems
   b. being a teenager is tough
   c. schoolwork is too difficult

Name _____ Date _____

● Reading Comprehension

Use with student book page 309.

A. Retell the story. Then tell whether or not you would recommend that your parents or other family members read "Hurricane Friends." Why or why not?

_____

_____

_____

_____

_____

_____

B. Write your response. How would you feel if you were in the house with the family in the story? How would you react to the situation?

_____

_____

_____

_____

C. Assess the reading strategy. How did describing mental images to yourself make the story more interesting?

_____

_____

_____

_____

Name _____ Date _____

● Spelling
Silent k Words

Use with student book page 309.

Some English words have silent letters. You need them to spell the word, but they are never pronounced. Some common examples are **knee** and **know**. Words starting with **kn-** always begin with an **n** sound. Look at the list of silent **k** words in the chart.

Verbs	**Knock** on the door. **Kneel** in front of the king. Did you **knead** the bread before you baked it? She **knits** sweaters every winter. Do you **know** the answer?
Nouns	We bought some useless **knickknacks**. Can I borrow your **knife**? Turn the **knob** and open the door. There was a single tree on the **knoll**. Can you untie this **knot**? Books contain a lot of **knowledge**. Can you bend your **knee**? The ring would not fit over my **knuckle**.

A. Circle the ten silent **k** words in this word search.

```
h   k   p   y   e   w   k   n   i   t
k   n   o   w   l   e   d   g   e   r
a   o   g   j   l   k   n   o   b   q
e   t   c   t   k   n   e   e   l   k
t   k   n   e   e   o   c   v   b   n
b   n   v   m   c   w   l   s   u   i
k   n   e   a   d   u   o   p   v   f
d   k   n   o   c   k   l   p   o   e
```

B. Write three sentences about your own life. Use a silent **k** word in each.

Example: _I had a knot in my shoelace this morning._

1. _____

2. _____

3. _____

Name _____ Date _____

● Writing Conventions
Writing Numbers with Hyphens

Use with student book page 309.

A hyphen (-) is a short line that is used in some words and word combinations. For example you might look for a **part-time** job. Hyphens are also used in many numbers. Here is how hyphens are used in numbers.

with cardinal numbers 20–99	twenty-one, twenty-two, etc.
with ordinal numbers	thirty-fifth, seventy-ninth, etc.

with fractions used as adjectives	When the fraction is used as an adjective before a noun, it has a hyphen.
	    Add **one-quarter** cup of flour.
	When a fraction is used as a noun to begin a sentence, it does not have a hyphen.
	    One half of the class was absent.

with descriptions of age	When you use number + *year* + *old* to describe someone's age, you use hyphens.
	    He was a **twelve-year-old** boy.
	    The **one-year-old** could already talk.

Rewrite the sentences as necessary. Use hyphens correctly. Write **correct** if the sentence is correct without hyphens.

Example: It was my twenty first birthday.

   It was my twenty-first birthday.

1. One third of the money is his. _____

2. Add one quarter teaspoon salt. _____

3. The two week old milk was bad. _____

4. Two thirds of us were sick that day. _____

5. He gave me one half of an orange. _____

6. He lives on the forty fifth floor. _____

7. That sixteen year old can run fast. _____

8. I need thirty three dollars more. _____

9. That is a six week old newspaper. _____

Name _____   Date _____

● Vocabulary Development
Shades of Meaning in Related Words

Use with student book page 311.

Synonyms are words that have the same meaning. However, some related words have small differences in meaning. These words have different shades of meaning.

Related Words	Related Meaning	Difference in Meaning	
regular ordinary	normal	**regular:** usual **ordinary:** common; not special	
damp soggy	wet	**damp:** a little wet **soggy:** wet and soft	
strong fierce	having physical strength	**strong:** having physical strength **fierce:** powerful, having great physical strength	

A. Complete each sentence with the correct word from the chart.

Example: The fire in the factory was _fierce_____.

1. The air feels _____ today.

2. He filled up the car with _____ gas.

3. I am lifting weights in order to become _____.

4. Water was dripping from the _____ sponge.

5. They gave me an _____ spoon, but I asked for a plastic spoon.

6. The lion looks _____ when it roars.

7. The ground was so _____ that I got water in my shoes.

8. The towel was not wet, but it was _____.

B. Use each of these pairs of words in a sentence that shows the meaning of the first word.

Example: (damp / cloth) _He took a damp cloth and cleaned the table with it._

1. (damp / sponge) _____

2. (soggy / shoes) _____

3. (strong / man) _____

4. (fierce / tiger) _____

Name _____ Date _____

● Grammar
Use with student book page 312.
Comparative Adjectives: -er and *more*

Use **-er** for most one-syllable adjectives.

Comparative Form of Adjectives: *-er*				
Subject	*be*	adjective + *-er*	*than*	
Tornadoes	are	smaller	than	hurricanes.

Use **more** for adjectives with two syllables or more.

Comparative Form of Adjectives: *more*				
Subject	*be*	more + adjective	*than*	
Hurricanes	are	**more** dangerous	than	regular storms.

Some adjectives have irregular comparative forms.
   good / better   **bad / worse**

A. Circle the correct adjective form.

Example: A hurricane is (more large / (larger)) than a thunderstorm.

1. Typhoons are (more violent / violenter) than thunderstorms.

2. Small storms sometimes combine to form a (more large / larger) storm.

3. The weather is (more calm / calmer) in the eye of a hurricane than outside it.

4. Some hurricanes are (more wide / wider) than 300 miles.

5. Some tornadoes are (more dangerous / dangerouser) than hurricanes.

6. During a hurricane, a house is a (gooder / better) place to stay than a car.

7. The basement is a (more safe / safer) place to stay than the first floor.

8. Tornado winds often are (more strong / stronger) than hurricane winds.

9. This car is (smaller / more small) than that truck.

10. This singer's songs are (popularer / more popular) than I thought they were.

Name _____ Date _____

B. Complete each sentence with the comparative form of the adjective in parentheses.

Example: I can run _____ faster _____ (fast) now than last year.

1. Math is _____ (difficult) than science for me.

2. My room is _____ (small) than my sister's room.

3. The weather is _____ (cold) in winter than in the fall.

4. Gary is _____ (tall) than his brother.

5. Mark is _____ (handsome) than Larry.

6. Fresh fruit is _____ (good) than canned fruit.

7. My father is _____ (old) than my mother.

8. News programs are _____ (interesting) than soap operas.

C. Write sentences using comparative adjectives. Use the words in parentheses.

Example: (inch / foot / short)

_____ An inch is shorter than a foot. _____

1. (lion / cat / dangerous)

_____

2. (tree / flower / tall)

_____

3. (grapes / apples / good)

_____

4. (magazines / newspapers / interesting)

_____

5. (spring / summer / cool)

_____

6. (milk / juice / expensive)

_____

Name _____ Date _____

● Grammar

Use with student book page 313.

Superlative Adjectives: -est and *most*

Use **-est** for most one-syllable adjectives.

Superlative Form of Adjectives: *-est*			
Subject	*be*	*the* + **adjective** + *-est*	
Antarctica	**is**	**the** cold**est**	place on Earth.

Use **most** for adjectives with two syllables or more.

Superlative Form of Adjectives: *most*			
Subject	*be*	*the* + *most* + **adjective**	
John	**is**	**the most** popular	student in the class.

Some adjectives have irregular superlative forms.
good / best   **bad / worst**

A. Circle the correct adjective form.

Example: It was (the more dangerous /(the most dangerous)) kind of storm.

1. Hurricane Andrew was (the most bad / the worst) hurricane of 1992.

2. The hurricane had (the most strong / the strongest) winds I have ever seen.

3. At 2:00, (the most fierce / the fiercest) winds began to blow.

4. The house was (the most dark / the darkest) during the middle of the storm.

5. The noise of the wind was (the most frightening / the more frightening) thing.

6. The wind was (the most loud / the loudest) at 3:00 A.M.

7. The rain was (the most heavy / the heaviest) just before the storm hit.

8. The basement was (the most soggy / the soggiest) part of the house.

9. The wind blew down (the tallest / more tallest) trees.

10. The storm damaged some of (the more important / the most important) buildings in town.

Name _____ Date _____

B. Complete each sentence with the correct superlative adjective form. Use an adjective in the box. Sometimes more than one answer is possible.

| ~~small~~   loud   delicious   bad   difficult   beautiful   interesting |

Example: My bedroom is _____*the smallest*_____ room in the house.

1. The grammar section was _____ part of the test.

2. That is _____ joke I have ever heard.

3. Barry has _____ voice of anyone in the class.

4. This is _____ book I have ever read.

5. This is _____ soup I have ever eaten.

6. Woods Parkway is _____ street in the city.

C. Complete the sentences with a comparative adjective or superlative adjective. Choose your own adjectives.

Example: New York City is _____*larger*_____ than Chicago.

1. History is _____ than biology.

2. My best friend is the _____ person I know.

3. Vacations are usually _____ than going to school.

4. My new clothes are _____ than my old ones.

5. Our school's baseball team is the _____ in the city.

6. English is one of the _____ classes for me.

7. Eating in a restaurant is _____ than eating in the cafeteria.

8. This year I am _____ than I was last year.

9. Tornados are one of the _____ kinds of storm.

10. Lions are _____ than rabbits.

11. Field trips are _____ than homework.

Name _____ Date _____

● **Writing Assignment**

Use with student book pages 314–315.

Personal Narrative: Write About a Storm

Use this chart to organize your ideas for your personal narrative.

1. First Paragraph	Where were you?
	_____
	How old were you?
	_____
	Who were you with?
	_____
	What were you doing before the storm hit?
	_____
	_____
2. Body	How did you find out about the storm?
	_____
	What preparations did you and others make?
	_____
	What was the storm like?
	_____
	_____
	How did you feel during the storm?
	_____
3. Final Paragraph	What happened after the storm?
	_____
	How did you feel?
	_____
	What did you and other people do?
	_____
	_____

Milestones A • Copyright © Heinle

Name _____   Date _____

● Writing Assignment
Writing Support

Use with student book page 315.

Mechanics: Commas

1. Use a comma between two or more adjectives that describe the same word but are NOT joined by the conjunction **and**.
   > It was a beautiful, sunny day.

2. Put commas between words or phrases in a series of three or more items.
   > She speaks, English, Spanish, French, and Italian.

A.   Rewrite these sentences. Use commas where necessary.

Example: They sold us some soft sweet delicious pears.

   _They sold us some soft, sweet, delicious pears._____

1.   We walked down the hall through the door and up the stairs.

   _____

2.   The car was long low and expensive.

   _____

3.   We relaxed on a nice big old sofa.

   _____

4.   I washed my face combed my hair and brushed my teeth.

   _____

B.   Use the words and phrases to write original sentences. Check your use of commas.

Example: (big / old / black)

   _A big, old, black bear crossed the road in front of us._____

1.   (down the sidewalk / through the gate / across the lawn)

   _____

2.   (windy / rainy / cold)

   _____

Name _____ Date _____

● Writing Assignment
Revising Activity

Use with student book page 315.

Use these exercises to practice your revision skills for a personal narrative. This narrative is about a teenager's first job.

1. When revising, be sure to present events in chronological order.

Number these events in chronological order.
_____ I decided to see if I could work at the bicycle shop on the corner.
_____ The owner said she might need help beginning in May.
___1___ I decided I needed to make some money of my own.
_____ I got my parents' permission to look for a job.

2. Always give background information.

Check the items that are important background information.
_____ The bicycle shop sells and repairs bikes.
_____ My father lost his job last year.
_____ I enjoy riding road bikes.
_____ I turned 16 last month.

3. Use descriptive words to create a vivid picture in the reader's mind.

Rewrite these sentences adding descriptive words.
• The bicycle shop is crowded.
_____
_____
• I was nervous.
_____
_____

Name _____ Date _____

● **Writing Assignment**

Use with student book page 315.

Editing Activity

A. Read this passage from a personal narrative and find the mistakes. Mark them using the editing marks on page 419 of your student book. Check the passage for the following items:

- the use of hyphens in numbers,
- the use of comparative,
- the use of superlatives,
- the use of commas,
- the spelling of words with a silent **k**,
- the use of words with different shades of meaning.

It was the colder day of the year. The temperature was about twenty two degrees F. It was also windiest day of the year. Under my coat I was wearing several layers: a T-shirt a flannel shirt and a sweater. I was also wearing long underwear and the warmer pants I own. Even with all those layers, my nees and toes were cold. However, I did not have any choice. I was in a contest to see who could get to the top of the mountain first. My team won, but when we got home, we were completely drowsy.

B. Make the corrections as you rewrite the journal entry.

_____

_____

_____

_____

_____

_____

_____

_____

Name _____ Date _____

● Vocabulary From the Reading

Use with student book page 332.

Key Vocabulary

custom	protection
loneliness	rude
pleased	weak
point	

A. Read the clues. Use the Key Vocabulary words to complete the puzzle.

Down

1. not polite
2. to indicate a place, direction, person, or thing, usually with a finger
3. a condition of being alone and feeling sad
4. feeling happy or satisfied
5. a regular practice that is special to a person, people, area, or nation

Across

4. action taken against harm or loss; a defense
6. not physically strong or not strong in character

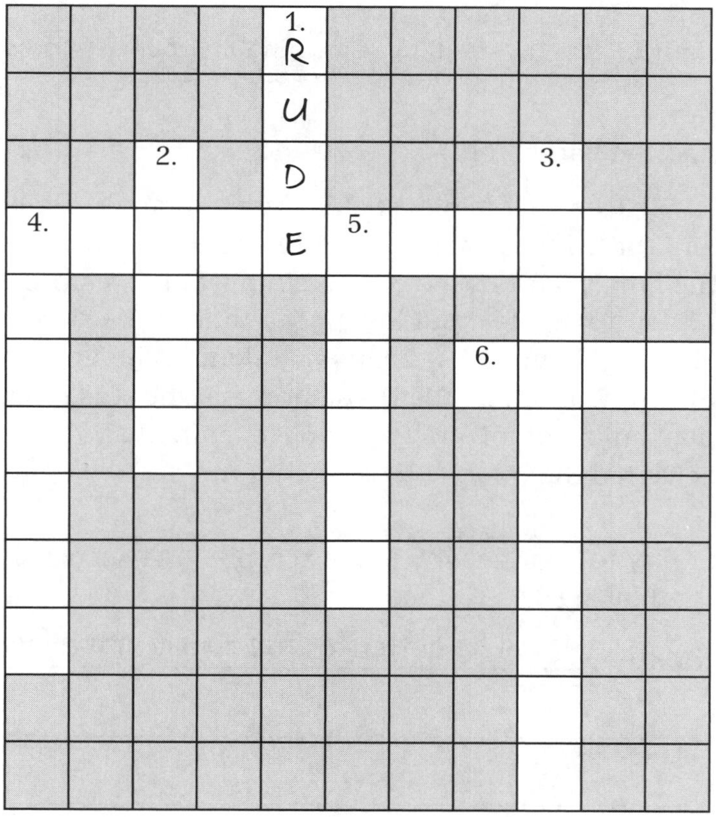

(crossword puzzle grid with 1. R, U, D, E spelling down)

B. The three Key Vocabulary words **pleased, weak,** and **rude** can be used to describe people. Use each one in a descriptive sentence of a person.

Example: The president was a weak leader so no one followed him.

1. _____

2. _____

3. _____

Name _____   Date _____

● Reading Strategy

Use with student book page 333.

Make Inferences

> When you **make** an **inference,** you make a guess based on information from the
> text and what you already know. When you **analyze** the text in this way, you get
> **insight** into it.

Academic Vocabulary for the Reading Strategy	
Word	**Explanation**
insight	the ability to see into or understand a complex person, situation, or subject
analyze	to examine something in order to understand what it means

Read the paragraph.

Bruce was the oldest child in a big family. He had two younger brothers
and three little sisters. His mother and his father both worked hard to support
the family, and Bruce worked in his father's store after school every day. His
father hoped he would work full-time at the store after high school. Of all the
children, Bruce was the most athletic. When he was in high school, he started
playing basketball. By his senior year, he was offered a basketball scholarship to
play on a big university team. He felt bad about disappointing his father, but he
accepted the offer.

A. Try to analyze why Bruce accepted the scholarship. What was he probably
thinking?

Example: _It will be better for the family in the long run if I go to college._

1. _____

2. _____

3. _____

B. As you look back at what you wrote in Exercise A, what insight do you find?
What kind of person is Bruce?

_____

_____

_____

Milestones A • Copyright © Heinle

Name _____ Date _____

● Text Genre
Novel

Use with student book page 334.

Novel	
character traits	a character's qualities; the kind of person the character is
character motivation	the reason a character does what he or she does
character changes	the ways a character becomes different as the story progresses

Read about Sandy. Then answer the questions.

Sandy was 13 years old when she took her first airplane trip. Her parents sent her to Canada to visit her grandmother. Sandy didn't want to go. She was shy and thought she wouldn't make any friends. She was also really scared of flying, and she was scared to be traveling all alone.

But things turned out better than she expected. She had a wonderful time in Canada. She loved being with her grandmother, and she met some great kids. She even found a new best friend, Carol. Now Sandy is back home, and she and Carol e-mail each other every day and talk about what they'll do together next summer. Now Sandy is counting the days until summer vacation and her next trip to Canada.

1. What are some of the traits of the character?

   She is shy. _____

   _____

   _____

2. How does the character change?

   _____

   _____

3. What is the motivation for these changes?

   _____

   _____

Name _____ Date _____

● **Reading Comprehension**   *Use with student book page 341.*

Academic Vocabulary for the Reading Comprehension Questions	
Word	**Explanation**
sequence	a connected series
judgment	the forming of an opinion after careful thought

A. Retell the story. As you retell the story, think back to Antonio's experience on his first day at school in *Bless Me, Ultima*. Relate this to your own experience. Describe the sequence of events you experienced on your first day of school.

_____

_____

_____

_____

_____

_____

B. Write your response. How did the other students treat Antonio? How do you feel about this? In your judgment, what should they have done?

_____

_____

_____

C. Assess the reading strategy. As you read *Bless Me, Ultima*, you were asked to make inferences. How does making inferences help you understand the story?

_____

_____

_____

_____

Name _____ Date _____

● Literary Elements

Use with student book page 341.

First-Person and Third-Person Narratives

> 1. In a first-person narrative, the narrator refers to himself or herself as **I**. Other characters in the story may be referred to as **he**, **she**, or **they**.
>
> 2. In a third-person narrative, the narrator is not a character in the story. All of the characters in the story are referred to by name or as **he**, **she**, or **they**.

A. This story is a third-person narrative. Rewrite it as a first-person narrative.

The alarm went off and Mike sat up in bed. He was so tired he could hardly open his eyes. He thought for a minute. He knew it was Saturday. He tired to remember why he had set the alarm. Then it came to him. He had a soccer game at 9:00 A.M. He had to be out of the house by 8:00.

The alarm went off and I sat up in bed. _____

_____

_____

_____

_____

B. This story is a first-person narrative. Rewrite it as a third-person narrative. The character telling the story is Luisa. Begin the story with her name.

It was my first day as a camp counselor. The children were beginning to arrive at Camp Playalot and the parents all wanted to talk to me. At 9:30, all the parents left and I called my group together for a meeting. They looked at me with wide eyes. Suddenly I realized that this was going to be a great summer.

_____

_____

_____

_____

Name _____ Date _____

● Vocabulary From the Reading

Use with student book page 342.

> **Key Vocabulary**
> climate   seasons
> divide

A. Write the Key Vocabulary word for each definition.

Word	Definition	
Example: ____seasons____	three-month periods of the year	
1. _____	the type of weather a region usually has	
2. _____	parts of the year with different weather	
3. _____	separate into parts	

B. Complete each sentence with one of the Key Vocabulary words.

Example: The year is divided into four ____seasons____.

1. Countries near the equator usually have a warm _____.

2. We used a bookcase to _____ our room into two halves.

3. My favorite of all the _____ is summer.

C. Describe the climate in the place where you live. What is the temperature like? Does it change a lot or stay the same? How much does it rain or snow?

_____

_____

_____

D. What season is it? What are the best and worst parts of this season?

_____

_____

_____

Name _____ Date _____

● Reading Strategy
Paraphrase

Use with student book page 343.

> When you **paraphrase**, you put part of a text in your own words.

Read the paragraph. Then rewrite the sentences in the chart in your own words.

    Ice climbing is a sport that in some ways resembles mountain climbing. However, instead of being on hard stone, ice climbers move up, down, and even across walls of cold, glassy ice. Climbers say that ice climbing can be very difficult and that it requires very serious attention. One of the difficult things about ice climbing is that the ice in one place can change from day to day, and even from hour to hour. The best way to go up a wall of ice in the morning may not be the best way to come down again later in the day. Ice climbers have to learn how to see differences in the face of the ice and change their plans accordingly.

Sentence	My Paraphrase
Ice climbing is a sport that in some ways resembles mountain climbing.	Ice climbing is like mountain climbing.
However, instead of being on hard stone, ice climbers move up, down, and even across walls of cold, glassy ice.	1. _____ _____ _____
One of the difficult things about ice climbing is that the ice in one place can change from day to day, and even from hour to hour.	2. _____ _____ _____
Ice climbers have to learn how to see differences in the face of the ice and change their plans accordingly.	3. _____ _____ _____

Name _____ Date _____

● Text Genre

Use with student book page 343.

Informational Text: Textbook

Textbook	
title	name of a reading
facts	information that can be proven
graphics	illustrations or charts that show information
captions	words that explain a picture or graphic

A. Read this passage from a textbook. Underline all the facts in the passage.

Disappearing Rain Forests

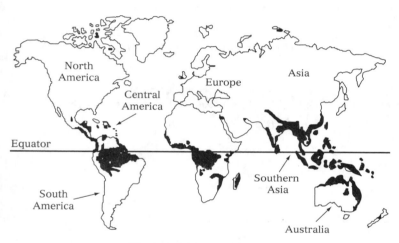

The World's Rain Forests

Many of us think of rain forests as beautiful, tropical places. We love to look at photos of the lush plant life and interesting birds and animals that live there. However, just as we are beginning to appreciate rain forests, they are starting to disappear at an alarming rate. Rain forests once covered 14% of Earth's land surface. Now they only cover about 6%. One and a half acres of rain forest are cut down every second. This is creating tremendous problems. Some scientists estimate that rain forests will be gone in less than 40 years.

B. Answer the questions. Use the text and graphic above.

1. What does the caption say?

_____

2. Are their any rain forests in Australia?

_____

3. Are there more rain forests north of the equator or south of the equator?

_____

Name _____ Date _____

● Reading Comprehension

Use with student book page 347.

A. **Summarize the reading.** In your summary, state what the difference is between a **biome** and an **ecosystem?** Give an example of a biome. Explain how one aspect of an ecosystem works.

_____

_____

_____

_____

_____

_____

_____

B. **Write your response.** Describe the biome and the ecosystem in which you live.

_____

_____

_____

_____

_____

C. **Assess the reading strategy.** How can paraphrasing help you understand scientific explanations like those in the reading "Biomes and Ecosystems?"

_____

_____

_____

_____

Name _____ Date _____

● **Spelling**   *Use with student book page 347.*
Silent *gh*

Some English words have silent letters. You need them to spell the words, but they are never pronounced. For example, the letters **gh** in the word **high** are not pronounced.

Look at the lists of silent **gh** words.

-igh words	*-ough* words	*-augh* words
bright	although	caught
fight	bought	daughter
high	brought	naughty
night	dough	slaughter
right	fought	
sight	through	
tight	thought	
weigh		

A. Answer the questions with a word containing the silent letters **gh.** You can use words from the lists above.

Example: What word means both **shiny** and **intelligent?** _bright_

1. What is the past tense of **fight?** _____

2. What do you call **uncooked bread?** _____

3. What is the opposite of **day?** _____

4. What is the opposite of **loose?** _____

5. If you do something **bad,** what are you? _____

6. What does a mother call her **female child?** _____

7. What is the past tense of **buy?** _____

8. What is the opposite of **wrong?** _____

B. Complete these sentences with a word that contains the silent letters **gh.**

Example: Yesterday I _____bought_____ an MP3 player at the mall.

1. When I walked outside, the sun was very _____.

2. Niagara Falls is a truly beautiful _____.

3. We went fishing and _____ three big fish.

4. We walked _____ the dining room and entered the kitchen.

5. I wanted to buy that dress, but the price was too _____.

238

Name _____ Date _____

● Writing Conventions
Use with student book page 347.

Punctuation: Commas, Semicolons, and Dashes

Here are some rules for using commas, semicolons, and dashes.

1. An adverbial clause at the beginning of a sentence is followed by a comma (,).

    When I got home, I took a nap.

2. Always put a comma between the day of the month and the year.

    September 7, 2007

3. A semicolon (;) can be used between two independent clauses when they are not joined by a coordinating conjunction.

    We got home late; I went straight to bed.

4. A dash (—) can be used to show a sudden break in a sentence.

    She managed to get home—I don't know how—before we did.

Rewrite these sentences adding commas, dashes, and semicolons.

Example: When the weather got cold I started wearing a sweater.

<u>When the weather got cold, I started wearing a sweater.</u>

1. There is one thing there are actually several things I need to say to you.

    _____

2. Before we went home we stopped at the library.

    _____

3. We looked in the closet it was empty.

    _____

4. Because it was raining I took my umbrella.

    _____

5. I told him listen to this that I didn't want the job.

    _____

6. As soon as they are ready my friends will join us.

    _____

7. I was born on June 12 1998.

    _____

8. Then Andrea what a disappointment decided to leave.

    _____

Name _____ Date _____

● Vocabulary Development

Use with student book page 349.

Frequently Used Foreign Words in English

> Many English words come from other languages. The words **chilis** and **tortillas** in the novel *Bless Me, Ultima* come from Spanish.

Look at the chart that shows some English words that come from other languages.

English Word	Language of Origin	Meaning
taco	Spanish	a corn tortilla filled with meat and vegetables
sushi	Japanese	rice rolled with fish and vegetables
spinach	Persian	a green, leafy vegetable
pizza	Italian	flat dough covered with tomatoes and cheese
croissant	French	a soft, flaky roll
enchilada	Spanish	a corn tortilla served in chili sauce
bagel	Yiddish	a doughnut-shaped roll with a hard crust
tea	Chinese	a hot beverage made with dried tea leaves
soy	Japanese	a kind of bean
pasta	Italian	noodles, macaroni, spaghetti

Complete each sentence with one of the English words above. Then tell which language it comes from.

Example: I like tomatoes, so I love _____*pizza*_____.

Language: _____*Italian*_____.

1. I don't like fish, so I never eat _____.

   Language: _____

2. My mother always has a cup of herbal _____ after dinner.

   Language: _____

3. My least favorite green vegetable is _____.

   Language: _____

4. He doesn't like hard rolls for breakfast; he prefers having a

   _____.

   Language: _____

5. I don't like chiles so I never order an _____.

   Language: _____

Name _____ Date _____

● Grammar
Use with student book page 350.

The Present Perfect Tense

> Use the **present perfect tense** to say that something happened in the past when the exact time is not important.
>> I **have** visited Spain and Italy.
>> She **has** read that book.
>
> Use the present perfect tense with **for** and **since** to talk about something that started in the past and continues to the present. Use **for** to talk about a period of time. Use **since** for a specific time.
>> John **has** lived in Florida **for** ten years.
>> They **have been** sick **since** Monday.

The Present Perfect Tense			
subject	has / have	past participle	
I / You / We / They	have	gone	to Europe.
He / She / It	has		

A.   Complete the sentences with the present perfect form of the verb in parentheses.

Example: She _____*has used*_____ (use) the new stove twice.

1. He _____ (dream) about becoming a movie star.

2. They _____ (want) to go swimming all summer.

3. She _____ (wait) hours for the bus every day this week.

4. He _____ (hate) eggs all his life.

B.   Complete these sentences using a present perfect verb form plus **for** or **since**.

Example: I _____*have lived*_____ (live) here _____*for*_____ two years.

1. Sue _____ (work) on her project _____ Monday.

2. I _____ (look) for you _____ 8:00.

3. Raoul _____ (wanted) a dog _____ six months.

4. The kids _____ (cook) every day _____ a week.

241

Name _____ Date _____

● Grammar Expansion

The Present Perfect Tense: Negative and Question Forms

The Present Perfect Tense: Negative			
subject	*has / have + not*	past participle	
I / You / We / They	**have not**	lived	in China.
He / She / It	**has not**		

A. Rewrite these sentences using the negative form of the present perfect tense.

Example: I have visited that museum. _____*I have not visited that museum.*_____

1. They have finished their homework. _____

2. She has cooked dinner. _____

3. We have talked to Mr. Blake. _____

4. You have cleaned your room. _____

The Present Perfect Tense: Question Form			
has / have	subject	past participle	
Have	I / you / we / they	waited	for a long time?
Has	he / she / it		

B. Read the answers. Then write the questions.

Example: ___*Have you used the computer?*___ Yes. I have used the computer.

1. _____ Yes. I have locked the door.

2. _____ No. I have not lived in Paris.

3. _____ Yes. He has waited for a long time.

4. _____ Yes. She has practiced the piano.

5. _____ No. I have not washed the dishes.

6. _____ Yes. They have read the books.

Name _____ Date _____

● Grammar

Use with student book page 351.

The Past Perfect Tense

> Use the **past perfect tense** to talk about one action or event that took place before
> another event took place in the past.
>   Antonio opened his lunch. (simple past)
>   Antonio's mother **had packed** his lunch earlier that morning. (past perfect)

The Past Perfect Tense			
subject	*had*	**past participle**	
I He / She You / We / They	**had**	studied	hard before the test.

A.   Underline the past perfect verbs in these sentences.

Example: I <u>had talked</u> with Nina before she went home.

1.   By the time I saw her, she had finished dinner.

2.   They had cleaned the kitchen when I got there.

3.   The teacher had waited for an hour by the time I arrived.

4.   Before I got home, the rain had stopped.

5.   We had washed our hands before we had lunch.

B.   Complete the sentences with the past perfect form of the verb in parentheses.

Example: Before breakfast, I _____*had worked*_____ (work) for an hour.

1.   They _____ (name) the baby Carlos before he was born.

2.   Before we left the store, we _____ (look) at several stereos.

3.   I _____ (care) for the baby all day, so I was really tired.

4.   They _____ (tell) their grandmother they loved her.

5.   She _____ (dream) about the tree several times.

6.   He _____ (smile) before he left.

Name _____ Date _____

● Grammar Expansion

The Past Perfect Tense: Negative and Question Forms

The Past Perfect Tense: Negative Form				
subject	*had not*	past participle		
I He / She You / We / They	**had not**	entered		the room.

A. Rewrite these sentences using the negative form of the present perfect.

Example: Bella had left by 2:00. _Bella had not left by 2:00._

1. The car had started right away. _____

2. Susan had cooked dinner. _____

3. Barry had liked playing cards. _____

4. She had asked to use my computer. _____

The Past Perfect Tense: Question Form				
had	subject	past participle		
Had	I he / she you / we / they	entered		the room?

B. Read the answers. Then write the questions.

Example: _Had you seen her before?_ Yes. I had seen her before.

1. _____ Yes. She had wanted to leave early.

2. _____ No. They had not practiced that morning.

3. _____ Yes. I had lived there for a long time.

4. _____ No. She had not washed her face.

Milestones A • Copyright © Heinle

Name _____ Date _____

● **Writing Assignment**
Business Letter: Write a Letter of Interest

Use with student book pages 352–353.

Use this page to help organize ideas for your letter of interest.

A. List some career choices that you have thought about. Then circle the one that you are most interested in.

B. List some organizations that do work related to the career choice you have circled.

C. Choose an organization to write to. Write the name and address of the organization here.

D. List several schools, activities, or experiences that would help make you become a good volunteer for this organization.

Name _____ Date _____

● Writing Assignment
Writing Support

Use with student book page 353.

> **Format: Format of a Business Letter**
> 1. When you write a business letter, make sure to include the following: your address, the full date, the address of the place you are writing to, a greeting, a colon (:) after the greeting, a closing, and your signature.
> 2. Be sure to capitalize: the month, the names of businesses and organizations, all first and last names and titles, the first letter of the greeting, and the first letter of the closing.

A. Label the parts of the business letter. Use the numbered list below.

1. closing	4. address of organization	6. body
2. greeting	5. ~~your address~~	7. signature
3. date		

___5___ 400 Rio Vista
San Antonio, TX 78258

_____ April 10, 2010

_____ AmeriCorps
1201 New York Avenue, NW
Washington, DC 20505

_____ Dear Sir or Madam:

_____ I am interested in learning more about the Learn and Serve America program. I have tutored young children in my school. I've also worked in an after-school day-care program. Please send me information about the program.

_____ Sincerely yours,

_____ *Anna Rodriguez*

B. Look at these instructions about business letters. Write **T** for **true** and **F** for **false**.

Example: __F__ Always abbreviate the date.

_____ 1. Use a comma after the greeting.

_____ 2. Capitalize the first letter of the greeting.

_____ 3. Capitalize the first letter of all words in the closing.

_____ 4. Capitalize the first word and all important words (nouns, adjectives, verbs) in the name of a business.

Name _____ Date _____

● Writing Assignment
Use with student book page 353.
Revising Activity

> **Revision Tips for a Letter of Interest**
>
> 1. Say exactly what volunteer work you want to do.
>
> 2. Include a clear statement of purpose—why you want to volunteer.
>
> 3. Include descriptions of some of your interests.
>
> 4. Include descriptions of work or other experience that relates to the job.
>
> 5. Use the present perfect tense to describe your interests and experience.

A. Look at this paragraph from a letter of interest. Make notes about things that need changing.

Doesn't say what you want to do.

I'm looking for a volunteer job at your hospital. I know you sometimes invite students to volunteer there. I am a sophomore at Bayside High School. I have a B+ average and I'm on the soccer team.

B. Rewrite the paragraph. Use the notes you made in Exercise A. Also use your ideas or the ideas in the box below.

> Your hospital has a big children's department.
> I want to be a nurse.
> I have babysat my neighbor's two children.
> I have read to them all the Harry Potter books.
> I have helped the kindergarten teacher at church.

_____

_____

_____

_____

_____

_____

_____

Name _____ Date _____

● Writing Assignment

Use with student book page 253.

Editing Activity

A. Read this letter of interest and find the mistakes. Mark them using the editing marks on page 419 of your student book. Check the letter for correct use of the items in the box.

1. capital letters	4. colons
2. abbreviations	5. the present perfect tense
3. commas	

36 Elm St.
Parkersburg, OH 44302

Mar. 13, 2010

Leonard's nursery
2100 Fourth Ave.
Greenwood, OH 44302

dear mr. Leonard,

I would like to volunteer to help out at your nursery on the weekends. I want to learn more about the business. I watered the lawn and raked the leaves since I was five years old. I also helped my father plant several trees. I am a hard worker and I hope I will be able to work for you.

Sincerely Yours:

Ricky Mason

B. Now rewrite the letter. Make the changes you marked above.

_____

_____

_____

_____

_____

_____

_____

_____

Milestones A • Copyright © Heinle

Name _____ Date _____

● Vocabulary From the Reading

Use with student book page 358.

Key Vocabulary

avoid	nation
familiar	roots
million	stranger

A. Write the Key Vocabulary word for each definition.

Word	Definition
Example: _____million_____	1,000,000 of something
1. _____	to stay away from so as not to do something
2. _____	an independent country with its own government
3. _____	connections to a place
4. _____	knowing about
5. _____	an unfamiliar person

B. Circle the correct word.

Example: Are you ((familiar) / stranger) with a food called borek?

1. I try to (avoid / roots) fast food.

2. There was a tall (nation / stranger) outside the door.

3. Over a (nation / million) people live in Detroit.

C. Answer the questions. Use a Key Vocabulary word in each answer.

Example: Do you spend time with unfriendly people?

   No, I avoid unfriendly people.

1. Where is your family from?

   _____

2. Do you know everyone in the supermarket?

   _____

3. How many people live in the United States of America?

   _____

Name _____   Date _____

● Reading Strategy
Summarize

Use with student book page 359.

> When you **summarize**, you give only the most important ideas of the reading in your own words. Use **brief** notes to help **organize** your thoughts.

Academic Vocabulary for the Reading Strategy		
Word	**Explanation**	
organize	to put in order, to arrange	
brief	short in length or time	

Summarize each passage below. Be sure to include the most important points in your summary.

1 My grandparents came to this country in 1936 and settled in New York. My grandfather worked as a porter in a hotel and my grandmother worked in a store. They both worked very hard and kept saving money. First, they lived in a single room downtown. Later, they moved to an apartment in the Bronx. Finally, after about ten years, they moved to a little town in New Jersey. That's where my parents were born and that's where I still live.

_____

_____

_____

2 My town is small, but it is growing fast. In 2005, ten thousand people lived here. In 2008, there were about thirteen thousand people here. That means that the population has grown by 10% each year. If the population growth continues at this rate for another five years, there will be almost about sixteen thousand people here. If this happens, I think we will have to build more schools and more houses and apartment buildings.

_____

_____

_____

Name _____ Date _____

● Text Genre

Use with student book page 360.

Primary Source Documents

Primary Source Documents	
types of primary source documents	diaries, letters, speeches, interviews
who creates them	people who lived during a certain time in history and who have direct knowledge of the events of that time
purpose for reading them	to help us understand the time in history when they were created

A. Tell what type of writing each primary source document is. Use the words **diary, letter, speech,** or **interview.**

Example: _____*speech*_____ You watch the president speaking on TV.

1. _____ You read what Abraham Lincoln wrote to a friend.

2. _____ You hear a TV reporter talking to Tom Cruise.

3. _____ You read what Columbus wrote while sailing to America.

B. Tell what type of primary source document you would use for each situation below. Use the words **diary, letter, speech,** and **interview.** Explain why you would use that particular document.

Example: You are researching everyday life in Boston in the 1800s.

I would want to read diaries of people living there in the 1800s because

they would include details of what life was like.

1. I would like to know what it was like for my uncle when he was in Vietnam.

_____

_____

2. You want to read the questions a magazine writer asked your favorite movie star and what his answers were.

_____

_____

Name _____ Date _____

● Reading Comprehension   *Use with student book page 367.*

Academic Vocabulary for the Reading Comprehension Questions		
Word	**Explanation**	
process	a series of actions that bring about a result	
authentic	real, not fake	

A. Summarize the reading. In your summary, include the processes some immigrants went through after arriving in the United States. Have you gone though any similar processes in your life?

_____

_____

_____

_____

_____

B. Write your response. What was your reaction to the immigrants' personal stories? Why do these stories feel so authentic?

_____

_____

_____

_____

C. Assess the reading strategy. How did summarizing the stories in this chapter help you understand and remember what the people experienced?

_____

_____

_____

_____

Name _____ Date _____

● Text Elements

Photos and Captions

Use with student book page 367.

> Informational texts about times in modern history often include **photos. Captions** are explanations of the photographs.

Write captions for the photos below.

Example:

A Passport Application

1.

_____

_____

2.

_____

_____

Name _____ Date _____

● Vocabulary From the Reading

Use with student book page 368.

Key Vocabulary	
bravery	patience
lot	soil

A. Write the Key Vocabulary word for each definition.

Word	Definition	
Example: ____lot____	area where a house is built	
1. _____	the ability to wait calmly	
2. _____	dirt or ground	
3. _____	courage, lack of fear	

B. Rewrite each sentence with a Key Vocabulary word.

Example: We want to plant trees in the empty space.
    We want to plant trees in the lot.

1. The earth in the garden was dark brown.

   _____

2. He showed great courage when the bear entered the campsite.

   _____

3. I showed my ability to wait calmly when the bus was two hours late.

   _____

C. Answer the questions. Use a Key Vocabulary word in each answer.

Example: What are firemen known for?
    They are known for their bravery.

1. What does a good farm have to have?

   _____

2. What is another way to say **an area of land**?

   _____

Name _____ Date _____

● Reading Strategy

Use with student book page 369.

Relate Your Own Experiences to a Reading

> If you **relate your experiences** to a character's experiences, you will understand the story better.

Read the following passage:

Anne had many hobbies. She liked to read, to collect postcards, and to make her own clothes. She studied a lot and got good grades. She was also on the swim team at school, and she played soccer with her friends on the weekend. She was always doing something. However, she sometimes wished she wasn't so busy. She thought about how nice it would be to sleep late. She dreamed about spending the entire weekend just being with her family. But somehow, she just couldn't do it. She just couldn't give up all her favorite activities.

A. Now relate your own experiences to those of the main character. Use a brief outline to organize you ideas.

How I'm similar to Anne:

_____

_____

_____

How I'm different from Anne:

_____

_____

_____

B. Now summarize the ways you are similar to and different from the character.

_____

_____

_____

_____

_____

Name _____   Date _____

● Text Genre
Novel

Use with student book page 369.

Novel		
character	a person in the story	
setting	where and when the story happens	
details and descriptions	details and descriptions help the reader imagine a story; this makes the story real and interesting	

Read this passage.

1 Linda loved the big, comfortable, old house where her family lived. She looked around her room. Everything was just perfect. Sun was streaming in through the soft white curtains. Her big blue and yellow pillows were scattered on the shiny wood floor. Just last night her friends had been lying on them, laughing and teasing each other. But this morning things are different. Something is wrong.

2 Linda's mother calls, "Linda, when are you going to get up. It's 9:00 already!" Linda says, "I'll be down in a few minutes, Ma." She looks around the room again. She picks up her diary and reads last night's entry. Then she shakes her head and puts the diary down. Slowly she gets up and walks out of the room into the hallway.

Complete the chart.

Features of the Novel	Examples from the Text	
1. characters	Linda	
2. setting		
3. third-person narrator		
4. details and descriptions		

Name _____ Date _____

● Reading Comprehension

Use with student book page 373.

A. **Retell the story.** In your retelling, answer these questions: Why did the girl plant beans in the vacant lot? How did the process of planting seeds and growing beans affect the people around her?

_____

_____

_____

_____

_____

_____

_____

B. **Write your response.** Relate your experiences to the girl in the story by answering these questions: Have you ever done anything you were afraid to do? Why did you do it? How did it turn out?

_____

_____

_____

_____

_____

C. **Assess the reading strategy.** How did relating your own experiences to the Vietnamese girl's story help you understand and remember the story better?

_____

_____

_____

_____

_____

Name _____ Date _____

● Spelling
Silent l

Use with student book page 373.

Some English words have silent letters. You need them to spell the words, but they are never pronounced. For example, there is a silent **l** in the word **folks**.

-alf Words	-alk Words	-ould Words	Proper Names
calf	chalk	could	Lincoln
half	talk	should	Stockholm
	walk	would	

A. Answer the questions with a word containing a silent **l**. You can use words from the list above.

Example: Which word is the name of a city? _____Stockholm_____

1. What is a baby cow? _____

2. What do you do when you say words? _____

3. What does your teacher write with on the board? _____

4. Who was the sixteenth president of the U.S.? _____

5. What word do you use to give advice? _____

6. What is the capital of Sweden? _____

7. What word do you use to ask permission? _____

8. What is one divided by two? _____

B. Complete these sentences with a silent **l** word from the list.

Example: Two quarters is the same as one ____half____.

1. The bus isn't running, so we have to _____.

2. There were a cow and a _____ on the farm.

3. If I were rich, I _____ buy a sports car.

4. The teacher dropped the _____ and it broke.

5. I need to _____ to you about the party tomorrow.

Name _____ Date _____

● Writing Conventions

Use with student book page 373.

Colons and Dashes

> **Colons with Lists**
> Use a colon to introduce a list.
> > We eat five meals a day: breakfast, lunch, and dinner.
>
> **Colons with Clock Time**
> Put a colon between the hour and the minutes.
> > 2:30
>
> **Dashes for Emphasis**
> When you interrupt a sentence to add very important information, place dashes before and after the added information.
> > Fast cars—ones that go more than 150 miles per hour—should not be allowed on public highways.

Rewrite these sentences adding colons or dashes.

Example: We left at 900 P.M.

_We left at 9:00 P.M._____

1. Please do the following. Get a newspaper, buy some milk, and feed the dog.

_____

2. The class started at 215.

_____

3. My grandfather he died last year was an excellent cook.

_____

4. We didn't get home until 145 A.M.

_____

5. There are three key ingredients. Olive oil, vinegar, and salt.

_____

6. They visited three countries last year, Mexico, Guatemala, and Belize.

_____

Name _____ Date _____

● Vocabulary Development
Use with student book page 375.

Denotative and Connotative Meaning

A word's denotative meaning is the meaning you find in the dictionary. A word's connotative meaning is the feelings you connect to the word.

A. Read each sentence. Write **T** for **true** and **F** for **false**.

Example: ____T____ The connotative meaning for **pet** is **friend**.

1. _____ A denotative meaning for **bone** is **part of the skeleton.**

2. _____ A connotative meaning for **dead** is **without life.**

3. _____ A denotative meaning for **money** is **comfort and security.**

4. _____ A connotative meaning for **vacation** is **fun and relaxation.**

5. _____ A denotative meaning for **heart** is **an organ that pumps blood.**

6. _____ A connotative meaning for **black cat** is **bad luck.**

B. Look at the underlined word in each sentence. Then write the **denotative** meaning of the word and some possible **connotative** meanings.

Example: All life ends in death.
Denotative meaning: _____the end of life_____
Possible connotative meanings: _____sadness; emptiness_____

1. We watched the <u>puppy</u> play.
Denotative meaning: _____

Possible connotative meanings: _____

2. We visited Jake in the <u>hospital</u>.
Denotative meaning: _____

Possible connotative meanings: _____

3. Linda wrote me a <u>poem</u>.
Denotative meaning: _____

Possible connotative meanings: _____

4. He gave her a bouquet of <u>roses</u>.
Denotative meaning: _____

Possible connotative meanings: _____

Name _____   Date _____

● Grammar

Use with student book pages 376–377.

Complex Sentences with Time Clauses

> Use complex sentences with time clauses to talk about an event and when the event happened in a single sentence. Use time words to clarify the order of events in a complex sentence.

Time Word	Meaning
before	earlier in time
after	later in time
when	at that time
while	during that time

A complex sentence is a sentence that includes a main clause and a subordinate clause.

A. Complete each sentence with the correct time word. There may be more than one correct answer for some sentences.

Example: You should study _____ *before* _____ you take the test.

1. I took a shower _____ I finished running.

2. _____ I was cooking dinner, I burned my hand.

3. The bell rang _____ I pushed the button.

4. _____ I took an aspirin, I felt a lot better.

5. I let the water warm up _____ I stepped into the shower.

B. Complete each sentence with a subordinate time clause with **before, after, when,** or **while.** Use true information if possible.

Example: I always drink hot chocolate _____ *when I am feeling cold* _____.

1. I always go home _____.

2. I sometimes have a snack _____.

3. Most people are nervous _____.

4. My parents are happy _____.

Name _____ Date _____

> Look at the punctuation used with subordinate time clauses.
>
> 1. When the sentence begins with the main clause, no comma is used.
>
>   My mother came to America when she was 16 years old.
>
> 2. When the sentence begins with the time clause, we put a comma at the end of the time clause.
>
>   Before she arrived in the U.S., she did not speak English.

C. Add commas to the sentences if necessary.

Example: When I won the race**,** I was really surprised.

1. We were tired when we got home from school.

2. After we got home we had a snack.

3. We watched TV while we ate our snacks.

4. Before I went out I cleaned my room.

5. They went to the library after they had lunch.

6. When they entered the library the librarian greeted them.

D. Combine the sentences. Use a comma where necessary.

Example: We closed the windows. We left.

_____We closed the windows_____ before _____we left_____.

1. The dog chewed up my shoe. I was at work.

   _____ while _____.

2. I got home. I was angry.

   When _____.

3. We went to the movie. We went to Joe's house.

   _____ before _____.

4. I looked up her number. I called her.

   After _____.

Milestones A • Copyright © Heinle

● Grammar Expansion

Complex Sentences with Other Kinds of Dependent Clauses

> A subordinate clause can describe a condition or a cause.
> **If you pay me,** I will help you.
> I will help you **because I like you.**

A. Combine these sentences using the conjunction given. Use commas as necessary.

Example: We ate a lot of apples. We were hungry. (because)

We ate _a lot of apples because we were hungry_.

1. We went home early. We missed the show. (because)

Because we went _____.

2. You can translate this. You know Spanish. (because)

You can _____.

3. Please take out the trash. You have time. (if)

Please _____.

4. It was hot. They opened the windows. (because)

Because _____.

5. You should read this book. You like science fiction. (if)

If _____.

B. Use the cues to write sentences with a main clause and a subordinate clause. Use **if** or **because** to begin the subordinate clause.

Example: I am hungry. _I am hungry because I didn't eat breakfast._

1. I won't stay up late. _____

2. It is too expensive. _____

3. I'll wear my raincoat. _____

4. We have a test tomorrow. _____

Name _____ Date _____

● Grammar Expansion

Compound Sentences with Two Independent Clauses

Another kind of sentence uses a **conjunction** to link two independent clauses.

Purpose of Second Clause	Conjunctions Used	Examples
to introduce a similar idea	**in addition** **in fact**	The shirt was ugly; **in addition**, it didn't fit. The weather was warm; **in fact**, it was hot.
to introduce an opposite idea	**however** **on the other hand**	I was tired; **however**, *we* went anyway. The music was good; **on the other hand**, it was extremely loud.

Look carefully at the punctuation used with these independent clauses.

  I like fruit; in fact, I love it.

  I can make dinner; however, it takes me a long time.

Notice that there is a **semicolon** before the conjunction, and there is a **comma** after it.

Combine these sentences using the conjunctions given. Use semicolons and commas.

Example: I don't like apples. I like pears a lot. (on the other hand)

  I don't like apples; on the other hand, I like pears a lot.
  _____

1. Our team is very good. We won every game last season. (in fact)

  _____

2. Orange juice is delicious. It's good for you. (in addition)

  _____

3. Linda loved the dress. She didn't buy it. (however)

  _____

4. That job sounds easy. It pays well. (in addition)

  _____

5. We could study for the test. We could go out. (on the other hand)

  _____

6. She swims well. She's an excellent swimmer. (in fact)

  _____

Name _____ Date _____

● **Writing Assignment**
Short Biography

Use with student book pages 378–379.

Use this chart to help organize your ideas for your short biography.

A. Choose a person to write about.

_____

B. Make notes about things you already know about the person.

_____

_____

_____

C. Prepare to interview the person. Write at least six questions you would like to ask the person.

1. _____

2. _____

3. _____

4. _____

5. _____

6. _____

D. Write the person's answers to the questions you asked.

1. _____

2. _____

3. _____

4. _____

5. _____

6. _____

Name _____ Date _____

● Writing Assignment

Writing Support

Use with student book page 379.

> **Mechanics: Direct Quotations**
> Direct quotations are a person's exact words.
>> Levine says, "I enjoy learning new things and meeting new people, even if they lived 200 years ago."

A. Rewrite the people's words in direct quotation form.

Example: Sarah: What are you doing?

Sarah asked, "What are you doing?" _____

1. Mr. Larson: Is this your book?

_____

2. Neil: You can sit here if you want.

_____

3. Mom: Have you taken your vitamins?

_____

4. The boss: Don't be late again!

_____

B. Change the sentences to direct quotations. Add capital letters and punctuation as needed.

Example: Allen asked what's in that box

Allen asked, "What is in that box?" _____

1. Sally said please sit over there

_____

2. Mahmood asked where is the cafeteria

_____

3. Kim shouted we're over here

_____

4. Luis said let's study later

_____